EFFECTIVE MINDSET CHANGE FOR LEADERS

TRANSFORMING ORGANIZATIONS THROUGH PERSONAL GROWTH

SCOTT E SALSBURY

Copyright © [2024] by Scott e Salsbury

All rights reserved. No part of this book may be reproduced, stored in a retrieval system, or transmitted in any form or by any means, electronic, mechanical, photocopying, recording, or otherwise, without the prior written permission of the publisher, except for brief quotations used in reviews or scholarly works.

Disclaimer: The information provided in this book is intended for educational and informational purposes only. The author and publisher are not engaged in rendering professional services. Readers are advised to seek professional guidance specific to their circumstances.Feel free to modify the details to fit the specific needs of your book.

TABLE OF CONTENTS

INTRODUCTION 5
CHAPTER 1 9
AWAKENING THE LEADER WITHIN 9

    BREAKING FREE FROM THE STATUS QUO: RECOGNIZING THE NEED FOR MINDSET TRANSFORMATION 14

    THE POWER OF SELF-AWARENESS: UNCOVERING BIASES AND ASSUMPTIONS 19

    EMBRACING VULNERABILITY: THE COURAGE TO LEAD AUTHENTICALLY 24

CHAPTER 2 31
REWIRING YOUR MINDSET 31

    FROM FIXED TO GROWTH: CULTIVATING A MINDSET OF CONTINUOUS LEARNING 37

    THE REFRAME REVOLUTION: CHANGING THE WAY YOU SEE AND OVERCOME CHALLENGES 42

    MINDFUL LEADERSHIP: TAMING EMOTIONAL REACTIVITY 50

    THE 5% RULE: OVERCOMING LIMITING BELIEFS AND MENTAL BARRIERS 57

CHAPTER 3 66
LEADING FROM THE HEART AND HEAD 66

    THE EMOTIONAL QUOTIENT OF

- LEADERSHIP: UNLOCKING YOUR COMPETITIVE EDGE ... 74
- LEADING WITH EMPATHY: BUILDING MEANINGFUL CONNECTIONS ... 82
- EFFECTIVE COMMUNICATION: SPEAKING WITH CLARITY AND COMPASSION ... 92
- RESOLVING CONFLICT WITH PURPOSE: TURNING TENSION INTO TEAMWORK ... 101

CHAPTER ... **110**
4 ... **110**
NAVIGATING COMPLEXITY AND CHANGE ... **111**

- RESILIENCE AND AGILITY: LEADING IN UNCERTAIN TIMES ... 117
- THE POWER OF PAUSE: MINDFUL DECISION-MAKING UNDER PRESSURE ... 122
- INNOVATION AND RISK-TAKING: CREATING A CULTURE OF EXPERIMENTATION ... 128
- SUSTAINABLE LEADERSHIP: CREATING A POSITIVE HERITAGE ... 135

CHAPTER ... **142**
5 ... **142**
SUSTAINING GROWTH AND MOMENTUM ... **143**

- MINDSET MAINTENANCE: BUILDING HABITS FOR LIFELONG GROWTH ... 153
- THE ROLE OF A SUPPORT NETWORK: SURROUNDING YOURSELF WITH POSITIVE INFLUENCERS ... 159
- OVERCOMING SELF-DOUBT: STRENGTHENING YOUR LEADERSHIP CONFIDENCE ... 164
- CELEBRATING SUCCESS: REINFORCING POSITIVE CHANGES ... 169

CHAPTER 6 — THE FUTURE OF LEADERSHIP 173

- THE EVOLVING LEADER: STAYING RELEVANT IN A RAPIDLY CHANGING WORLD 182
- LEADING WITH PURPOSE: ALIGNING MINDSET WITH CORE VALUES 189
- CREATING A MINDFUL LEADERSHIP CULTURE: INSPIRING POSITIVE CHANGE 194
- THE MINDSET LEGACY: SHARING YOUR WISDOM WITH FUTURE GENERATIONS 201

CONCLUSION 206

- THE MINDSET REVOLUTION: TRANSFORMING LEADERS, TRANSFORMING ORGANIZATIONS 209

INTRODUCTION

In the crucible of ancient wars, leaders were often measured not by their physical might, but by their capacity to adapt.

A renowned ancient conqueror, barely twenty years old, transformed from a student under a famed Greek philosopher into a leader who reshaped the world map.

His unmatched ability to shift his mindset—embracing new strategies, aligning with diverse cultures, and inspiring loyalty—was the secret to his enduring legacy.

History teaches us that great leaders are not born; they are forged in the fires of change and adaptability.

Consider the story of a tech CEO navigating the chaos of a disrupted industry. Initially resistant to change, the company teetered on the brink of collapse until the leader embraced a transformational shift.

By adopting innovative thinking, empowering their team, and pivoting to new opportunities, they not only saved the company but turned it into a market leader.

This real-world example demonstrates that mindset change isn't just theoretical; it's the cornerstone of sustained leadership success.

Leadership is no longer about sticking rigidly to what worked yesterday—it's about evolving to meet the demands of today and tomorrow.

The greatest leaders possess an unparalleled ability to reshape their thinking, leaving behind old paradigms and embracing growth.

Effective mindset change isn't a soft skill; it's a critical tool for any leader aiming to thrive in a rapidly changing world.

Whether you lead a team of ten or ten thousand, the strategies in this book will help you unlock your potential, inspire your people, and drive your vision forward.

This book is your comprehensive guide to transformation, offering practical advice and expert insights to help you achieve your goals.

It's time to redefine what leadership means in your life, master the art of mindset change, and unleash the leader you were meant to be.

Is now the moment for you to rise above the obstacles that have been holding you back and achieve your goals?

Ready to unlock your full leadership potential and lead with precision, passion, and impact?

This book is your guide to mastering the most critical shift of your leadership journey.

Don't just read about transformation—experience it. Open these pages, and let's embark on the path to becoming a leader who not only adapts but thrives. Your next chapter of leadership starts here.

CHAPTER

1

AWAKENING THE LEADER WITHIN

What separates great leaders from average ones?

The answer lies not in innate talent but in the ability to adopt an effective mindset that fosters adaptability, resilience, and vision.

Leadership is a mindset and a behavior, not just a title or position; it's about the actions you take and the impact you make.

The best leaders understand that their mindset dictates their capacity to influence others, navigate challenges, and create meaningful change.

Without the right mindset, even the most skilled leader can fall short of their potential.

A company on the brink of collapse due to a sudden industry shift places its hope in a new manager.

This leader doesn't arrive with groundbreaking technical knowledge or a miraculous strategy.

Instead, they focus on reshaping the team's perspective, fostering an environment of possibility, and guiding them toward innovative solutions.

Within months, the company not only stabilizes but begins to thrive, outpacing its competitors. The turning point? A leader who understood that mindset is the foundation of transformation.

Leaders are not born; they are crafted through experience, self-awareness, and a deliberate shift in mindset.

To awaken the leader within, you must challenge preconceived notions, unlearn unproductive habits, and embrace a growth-oriented outlook.

1. Shift from Scarcity to Abundance

Many leaders operate from a place of fear—fear of losing resources, opportunities, or relevance.

Effective leaders understand that focusing on possibilities rather than limitations leads to creativity and solutions. This shift enables you to see opportunities where others see roadblocks.

2. Prioritize People Over Processes

While processes and systems are essential, true leadership is about inspiring and empowering people.

Adopting a mindset that values connection and collaboration unlocks team potential and builds trust, resulting in better outcomes.

3. Embrace Continuous Learning

An effective leader recognizes that the world is ever-evolving. Cultivate a mindset of curiosity and humility, where every challenge is an opportunity to learn and grow.

This adaptability ensures you remain relevant and effective, regardless of external circumstances.

4. Lead with Purpose

A powerful mindset stems from clarity of purpose. Leaders who align their actions with a greater mission inspire those around them and create a ripple effect of positivity and productivity.

5. Resilience Over Perfection

Mistakes are inevitable. Effective leaders focus on recovering from setbacks rather than avoiding them.

A resilient mindset fosters persistence, turning failures into stepping stones for success.

BREAKING FREE FROM THE STATUS QUO: RECOGNIZING THE NEED FOR MINDSET TRANSFORMATION

When we encounter a groundbreaking concept, our minds undergo a permanent transformation, expanding our potential for growth and exploration.

Picture driving in a dense fogbank, where the only visible horizon is a few feet in front of you.

The road ahead is unclear, and despite your best efforts, you're hesitant to accelerate.

Suddenly, the sun breaks through, dissipating the mist and revealing a stunning, open highway.

The clarity encourages you to drive faster, make bolder turns, and enjoy the journey.

This is what breaking free from the status quo feels like—a mental fog lifting to reveal untapped potential and opportunities for growth.

Leadership is that open highway, but only for those who are ready to shed their limiting beliefs.

In the realm of leadership, the status quo is a tempting comfort zone. It offers familiarity and predictability but often at the expense of innovation and progress.

Effective leaders understand that staying stuck in old ways of thinking—whether it's clinging to traditional methods of resisting change—limits their ability to inspire and achieve.

The need for mindset transformation begins with recognizing that the world is constantly evolving. Markets shift, technology advances, and team dynamics adapt.

Leaders must be willing to transform and grow alongside their organizations; otherwise, they risk losing their edge and becoming outdated.

Consider how companies that resisted digital transformation were overshadowed by those that embraced it. The same principle applies to leadership: transformation isn't optional; it's essential.

True innovation requires a willingness to challenge and redefine the deeply held beliefs and assumptions that underpin the existing order.

Are you holding onto practices that no longer serve your team? Are you resisting new ideas out of fear or habit? The first step to effective mindset change is self-awareness—acknowledging that growth begins when comfort ends.

Once this awareness is achieved, the focus shifts to intentional action. Leaders must cultivate curiosity, seek diverse perspectives, and embrace a willingness to unlearn and relearn.

This path isn't for the faint of heart; it demands ego surrender and a willingness to be vulnerable in pursuit of growth.

However, the reward is immense: a renewed sense of purpose, increased team morale, and the ability to navigate challenges with resilience.

Mindset transformation also influences organizational culture. When leaders model adaptability and openness, it cascades down to their teams, creating an environment where innovation thrives.

Breaking free from the status quo is not just a personal journey but a collective one, fostering a culture of continuous improvement.

In essence, mindset transformation is the foundation of effective leadership. It's the catalyst that propels leaders out of the fog and into the clarity of visionary thinking.

Your mindset as a leader determines the scope and scale of the impact you can have.

It's time to embrace the change, step into the unknown, and lead with renewed purpose.

THE POWER OF SELF-AWARENESS: UNCOVERING BIASES AND ASSUMPTIONS

When we turn inward to understand ourselves, we uncover the silent architects of our perceptions—our biases and assumptions—allowing us to lead with clarity and purpose.

Visualize a leader guiding their team through uncharted and foggy terrain, requiring agility, adaptability, and clear vision.

The compass is slightly misaligned, and the map carries faded, handwritten notes from previous captains.

The journey begins confidently, but with time, it becomes clear: the ship is veering off course. Self-awareness is the light that pierces the fog, the recalibration of the compass, and the erasure of outdated notes.

Without it, even the most skilled navigator cannot avoid unseen obstacles. Leaders, much like captains, must clear their mental tools of biases and assumptions to chart a successful course.

Effective leadership starts within. Self-awareness is not just a trendy concept; it is the foundation of impactful leadership.

To guide others effectively, leaders must first recognize the internal narratives shaping their decisions and interactions.

This process involves identifying personal biases, challenging long-held assumptions, and cultivating an openness to new perspectives.

Biases are the mental shortcuts we often rely on to make decisions quickly, but they can cloud judgment.

For instance, confirmation bias—a tendency to favor information that aligns with our beliefs—can lead leaders to dismiss valuable input from their team.

Similarly, assumptions can create blind spots, preventing leaders from seeing opportunities or risks that challenge the status quo.

Uncovering these internal obstacles requires intentional self-reflection. Tools like journaling, seeking honest feedback from colleagues, and engaging in mindful practices can illuminate areas where biases and assumptions operate.

This practice not only sharpens decision-making but also enhances emotional intelligence—a vital skill for navigating complex interpersonal dynamics.

Self-awareness also fosters a growth mindset. Leaders who embrace the discomfort of confronting their mental habits cultivate resilience and adaptability.

By recognizing that they do not have all the answers, they create an environment where learning and innovation thrive.

When leaders take the time to understand themselves, they unlock a powerful ability to connect authentically with their teams.

They become role models of introspection and humility, inspiring others to do the same.

In a world where change is constant, the leader who embraces self-awareness gains an edge—not just in strategy but in fostering a culture of trust and collaboration.

Self-awareness is the rudder that keeps leadership steady amid uncertainty. By addressing biases and assumptions, leaders pave the way for effective mindset change, unlocking their full potential and empowering those they lead.

EMBRACING VULNERABILITY: THE COURAGE TO LEAD AUTHENTICALLY

A true leader is not the one who hides behind a facade of perfection but the one who steps forward with authenticity, embracing their flaws as the bridge to connection and growth.

Leadership is often seen as a demonstration of strength, competence, and unshakable confidence.

However, history and experience reveal a deeper truth: the most impactful leaders are those who have the courage to embrace vulnerability.

Far from being a weakness, vulnerability is a powerful asset that fosters trust, innovation, and meaningful relationships.

- **The Transformation of Leadership Mindsets**

Traditionally, leadership has been equated with authority and invincibility, often discouraging the display of emotions or personal challenges.

This approach, rooted in industrial-era practices, prioritized rigid structures over human connection.

However, as leadership theories evolved, influential thinkers like a renowned research professor on shame and vulnerability and a celebrated management consultant highlighted a paradigm shift—effective leaders must lead with heart, authenticity, and openness.

This shift not only changes how leaders see themselves but also transforms their teams and organizations.

Take, for example, the 16th President of the United States. Often celebrated for his wisdom and resolve, this iconic American leader also openly acknowledged his moments of doubt and grief, especially during the nation's most divisive conflict.

By sharing his struggles, he inspired those around him to trust and rally behind his vision. His vulnerability didn't diminish his leadership but reinforced his humanity, making his influence timeless.

- **Beyond the Facade: The Importance of Vulnerability in Effective Leadership**

To lead authentically is to shed the armor of perfection. When leaders embrace vulnerability, they invite collaboration and creativity.

Teams are more likely to take risks, share ideas, and work toward collective goals when they see their leaders acknowledging mistakes and expressing genuine emotions.

Vulnerability builds a culture of psychological safety, which research has shown is a cornerstone of high-performing teams.

The story of the former CEO of a renowned global coffeehouse chain, who led the company's transformative turnaround, underscores this principle.

During challenging times, he openly admitted to employees that mistakes had been made and sought their input to rebuild the brand's culture.

His willingness to show humility and involve others in the process not only restored the company's growth but also cemented his reputation as a leader who valued people over pride.

Mindset change among leaders requires an intentional pivot from self-protection to self-awareness.

This is evident in the leadership of India's iconic independence leader. His approach to leading the country's freedom movement demonstrated an unparalleled combination of humility and vulnerability.

Rather than adopting the tactics of power-driven leaders, he embraced simplicity, shared his personal struggles, and connected deeply with the people he served.

His ability to change his mindset—to lead through service and transparency—was key to uniting millions under a common cause.

- **Vulnerability in Leadership: A Step-by-Step Implementation Guide**

1. **Acknowledge Imperfection:** Recognize that no one has all the answers. Show your team that growth is a lifelong process by openly sharing your own learning and development journey.

2. **Listen Actively:** Show genuine interest in the perspectives of others, even when it challenges your own.

3. **Own Your Mistakes:** When errors happen, admit them openly and focus on solutions rather than deflection.

4. **Share Your Story:** Let your team know the experiences that shaped your leadership journey, including setbacks and triumphs.

- **Why Authenticity Matters for Effective Mindset Change**

Authenticity transforms leadership into a shared journey rather than a solitary mission.

Leaders who embrace vulnerability and lead authentically unlock their team's potential by creating an environment where people feel seen and valued.

This shift in mindset doesn't just improve leadership outcomes; it humanizes the workplace, building resilience and trust in the process.

In a world that increasingly values connection over control, the courage to lead authentically is not just a choice but a necessity.

As leaders step into their true selves, they inspire others to do the same, paving the way for collective success and enduring impact.

CHAPTER

2

REWIRING YOUR MINDSET

What Does It Take to Transform Your Leadership Potential?

What if the only thing standing between you and exceptional leadership was a shift in your mindset?

How often do you find yourself stuck in old habits, unable to inspire your team or adapt to changing circumstances?

These are questions every leader must face. True leadership isn't just about strategies or skills; it's about adopting a mindset that embraces growth, resilience, and innovation.

The most successful leaders understand that transformation starts within. They challenge their assumptions, let go of limiting beliefs, and open themselves to new possibilities.

But how do they do it? The answer lies in rewiring their mindset. It's not just about thinking differently; it's about cultivating a leadership philosophy that fuels personal growth and empowers teams to excel.

Rewiring your mindset as a leader is not a one-time act; it is an ongoing process of reshaping your perceptions, behaviors, and responses to challenges.

Here are the key steps to cultivating an effective mindset change for leaders:

1. Shift From Fixed Thinking to Growth-Oriented Thinking

Leaders who adopt a growth mindset see failures as stepping stones for success, using each setback as a chance to learn, adjust, and move forward.

They view challenges as catalysts for innovation and foster a culture that values experimentation, learning, and continuous growth.

When faced with a setback, begin by asking yourself: 'What opportunity for growth and learning is hidden within this challenge?" A growth mindset enables you to reframe challenges as catalysts for innovation, learning, and progress, helping you unlock your full potential and achieve your vision.

2. Embrace Emotional Intelligence

Understanding your own emotions and those of others is a critical part of leadership.

A rewired mindset prioritizes empathy, active listening, and effective communication. These qualities help build trust and motivate your team to perform at their best.

3. Reevaluate Your Definition of Success

Instead of focusing solely on results, successful leaders prioritize the process and relationships that lead to those results. This shift helps sustain long-term success, even in the face of adversity.

4. Adopt a Servant Leadership Perspective

A transformed leader views their role not as one of authority but as one of service.

Supporting your team members, understanding their needs, and removing barriers to their success creates a collaborative and productive work environment.

5. Commit to Lifelong Learning

Great leaders never stop learning. They read, network, and expose themselves to diverse perspectives.

This continuous expansion of knowledge and experience enables them to stay ahead in a fast-changing world.

- **Making the Connection**

A leader's mindset is the foundation upon which their influence is built, determining the depth and breadth of their impact.

By asking yourself powerful questions about your current approach and committing to rewiring how you think, you unlock new possibilities for personal and professional growth.

Each of the steps outlined here is a building block for creating a mindset that not only enhances your leadership potential but also inspires those you lead to strive for excellence.

Rewiring your mindset is the bridge between where you are and where you want to be as a leader.

Begin today by challenging your own thoughts and daring to think differently. The rewards of this transformation—greater influence, deeper connections, and lasting success—are well worth the effort.

FROM FIXED TO GROWTH: CULTIVATING A MINDSET OF CONTINUOUS LEARNING

Leadership is a catalyst for growth, empowering individuals to reach their full potential and driving collective success.

In today's fast-paced, ever-evolving world, leaders are no longer judged solely by their expertise but by their ability to adapt, inspire, and foster innovation.

The key to this lies in mindset. For too long, many have clung to outdated, rigid beliefs that stifle progress.

But true leadership begins with the courage to challenge one's thinking and embrace a mindset primed for growth and continuous learning.

The most successful leaders aren't those who know everything but those who remain curious, resilient, and open to new possibilities.

They understand that their influence grows as they grow. So, how can leaders shed limiting perspectives and adopt a mindset that transforms not just their leadership but also their teams and organizations?

The journey begins with moving from a fixed mindset to a growth mindset—a shift that changes everything.

A fixed mindset views abilities and intelligence as static traits, creating an environment where fear of failure prevails.

Leaders with this perspective often avoid risks, resist feedback, and prefer the comfort of what is already known.

While this approach may provide short-term stability, it limits long-term success by suppressing innovation, adaptability, and collaboration.

A growth mindset, on the other hand, embraces challenges as opportunities for development.

It thrives on feedback, sees failure as a stepping stone to improvement, and fosters a culture where creativity and resilience flourish.

Leaders who adopt this mindset inspire trust, nurture potential, and drive meaningful change. To cultivate this mindset, leaders must:

1. Embrace Vulnerability: Acknowledge that you don't have all the answers and that learning never stops. By showing humility, you encourage others to do the same.

2. Prioritize Feedback: Welcome constructive criticism as a tool for self-improvement. Use it to refine your strategies and enhance your impact.

3. Encourage Experimentation: Create an environment where calculated risks are supported. This not only boosts innovation but also empowers your team to think boldly.

4. Celebrate Growth: Recognize progress—yours and others'—no matter how small. This reinforces the value of perseverance and continuous effort.

5. Stay Curious: Commit to lifelong learning. Read, network, and explore areas outside your expertise to expand your perspective.

As leaders make this shift, they model a powerful example for their teams. They demonstrate that growth is not just possible—it's essential.

This transformation radiates throughout organizations, creating a ripple effect that drives collaboration, innovation, and sustainable success.

True leadership begins with a willingness to grow. When leaders cultivate a growth mindset, they don't just lead—they elevate. It's not just about changing strategies; it's about changing lives—starting with your own.

THE REFRAME REVOLUTION: CHANGING THE WAY YOU SEE AND OVERCOME CHALLENGES

True leadership is not about avoiding challenges but transforming them; it is the art of reframing obstacles into opportunities, setbacks into lessons, and uncertainties into pathways for growth.

The leader who masters this mindset does not just inspire others—they create a culture where resilience thrives, innovation flourishes, and every adversity becomes a stepping stone to greater achievement.

Leadership is often a journey through uncharted territory. The ability to navigate obstacles with clarity and vision defines effective leaders.

One of the most powerful tools in a leader's arsenal is reframing—shifting perspectives to see challenges as opportunities.

Reframing is not just a cognitive exercise; it is a transformative mindset that empowers leaders to lead with purpose and resilience.

- **Understanding Reframing**

Through reframing, we can reorient our thinking, challenge our assumptions, and develop a more constructive and hopeful perspective on life's challenges.

Instead of seeing challenges as insurmountable problems, leaders can redefine them as opportunities for growth, innovation, or strategic advantage.

This mental shift allows for creative problem-solving and helps in fostering a culture of optimism within teams.

For instance, consider a project that is failing due to unforeseen circumstances.

A leader adept at reframing might view this setback as a chance to identify weaknesses in current strategies, improve processes, and strengthen team dynamics for future success.

- **Why Reframing Matters for Leaders**

1. Encourages Innovation:

When faced with obstacles, teams are often compelled to rethink their strategies, leading to the development of fresh perspectives and innovative ideas.

By reframing setbacks as opportunities for innovation, leaders can inspire their teams to explore creative solutions that may not have been considered otherwise.

2. Builds Resilience:

The ability to see a silver lining in adversity strengthens mental and emotional resilience. Leaders who reframe effectively demonstrate to their teams that setbacks are temporary and surmountable, fostering a positive organizational culture.

3. Promotes Growth:

When leaders view obstacles as learning opportunities, they model a growth mindset.

This encourages individuals and teams to embrace change, take risks, and develop new skills, leading to overall organizational progress.

- **Practical Steps to Reframe Challenges**

1. Shift Your Language:

Words shape perception. Replace negative phrases like "This is a problem" with empowering ones like "This is an opportunity to improve." Language reframing sets the tone for how others approach challenges.

2. Focus on the Bigger Picture:

Step back and assess the broader impact of the challenge. Ask questions like, "How can we use this experience as a springboard for growth, experimentation, and discovery?" or "How does this experience support our overarching objectives and long-term vision?"

This more expansive viewpoint allows you to see beyond the immediate challenge, revealing the potential benefits and opportunities that arise from adversity.

3. Engage Diverse Perspectives:
Collaboration can bring fresh insights. Encourage your team to share their viewpoints on the challenge.

Often, new ideas emerge when multiple perspectives are combined, turning the obstacle into a collaborative opportunity.

4. Practice Emotional Detachment:
Leaders who remain emotionally grounded can reframe situations more effectively.

Take a moment to separate your feelings from the challenge at hand. This clarity allows for objective decision-making and helps maintain focus on solutions.

5. Celebrate Small Wins:

Even in adversity, there are victories. Acknowledging progress, no matter how minor, keeps morale high and reinforces the mindset that challenges can be overcome.

- **Real-Life Example of Reframing**

One of the most notable examples of reframing in leadership comes from industries that faced massive disruption.

When digital transformation disrupted traditional retail, many companies struggled.

However, leaders who embraced the shift viewed it as an opportunity to innovate.

Brands that invested in e-commerce, streamlined supply chains, and enhanced customer experiences not only survived but thrived, setting new standards for the industry.

- **The Transformational Impact of Reframing**

Reframing is more than just a leadership skill; it is a transformative way of thinking. It enables leaders to turn roadblocks into stepping stones, building a legacy of adaptability and success.

By adopting this mindset, leaders create a ripple effect that influences their teams and organizations, empowering everyone to rise above challenges.

In the dynamic world of leadership, where uncertainty is inevitable, mastering the art of reframing equips leaders with the ability to thrive.

Challenges will always exist, but how we view and respond to them determines our ultimate success.

MINDFUL LEADERSHIP: TAMING EMOTIONAL REACTIVITY

Leadership is a dual-edged sword, requiring the ability to make tough decisions while also empathizing with and managing the emotions of team members.

Emotional reactivity, if left unchecked, can lead to impulsive actions, strained relationships, and diminished trust within teams.

Mindful leadership offers a powerful pathway to taming emotional reactivity and fostering an effective mindset change.

By cultivating awareness, self-regulation, and intentionality, leaders can transform their approach to challenges and inspire others to do the same.

- **The Challenge of Emotional Reactivity in Leadership**

Emotional reactivity occurs when emotions, rather than rational thinking, drive decisions and actions.

It might manifest as frustration in meetings, defensive responses to feedback, or even avoidance of difficult conversations.

While human emotions are natural, allowing them to dictate leadership behavior often undermines long-term goals.

- **The Role of Mindfulness in Leadership**

At its core, mindfulness is about embracing the present moment, free from judgment, and cultivating awareness of your thoughts, emotions, and surroundings. For leaders, mindfulness equips them to:

1. Pause Before Reacting: Instead of responding impulsively, mindful leaders create a moment of pause to assess their emotional state and the situation objectively.

2. Understand Emotional Triggers: Mindfulness helps leaders identify recurring triggers that lead to reactivity, enabling proactive management.

3. Cultivate Emotional Resilience: A mindful approach enhances emotional resilience, ensuring that leaders maintain composure during crises.

- **Steps to Taming Emotional Reactivity**

1. Self-Awareness

Recognize your emotional patterns. Journaling or reflecting on past interactions can help identify moments where emotions overtook rationality.

Awareness is the first step towards transformation, allowing us to recognize and replace limiting patterns with more empowering and conscious choices.

2. Breath Control

Simple breathing exercises can anchor you in the present moment and calm intense emotions.

Diaphragmatic breathing is a potent tool for activating the parasympathetic nervous system, promoting relaxation, and mitigating the effects of stress and anxiety.

3. Reframe Perspectives
Train yourself to view challenges as opportunities for growth rather than threats. Reframing minimizes stress and reduces emotional intensity.

4. Set Intentions
Start your day with clear intentions, such as "I will lead with patience and compassion today."

These intentions act as a mental guide, helping you remain steady even when emotions arise.

5. Practice Regular Reflection

At the end of each day, evaluate your emotional responses. Reflecting on what went well and what could improve reinforces positive behavior.

- **Mindful Leadership in Action**

Consider a leader faced with an underperforming team member. Emotional reactivity might lead them to express anger or disappointment in a way that demotivates the individual.

However, a mindful leader would pause, evaluate the situation, and approach the conversation with empathy, focusing on constructive feedback. Such an approach not only resolves the issue but also strengthens trust.

For those looking to explore the principles of mindfulness and emotional mastery in greater depth, my book, **Mindful Living Essentials**, offers practical insights and strategies tailored for both personal and professional growth.

It serves as a companion to this discussion, providing actionable steps to embrace mindfulness as a way of life.

I encourage you to get a copy for yourself and experience the transformative power of mindful living firsthand.

- **Transforming Leadership Through Mindfulness**

Mindful leadership is not a fleeting trend but a foundational skill for navigating the complexities of modern leadership.

By taming emotional reactivity and fostering a mindset of clarity, leaders can unlock their potential and inspire their teams to achieve greatness.

Embracing mindfulness is not just about managing emotions; it's about leading with purpose, authenticity, and unwavering focus.

THE 5% RULE: OVERCOMING LIMITING BELIEFS AND MENTAL BARRIERS

True transformation begins not in the grand leaps, but in the quiet, consistent steps we take to challenge our doubts and expand our boundaries.

The smallest shift in mindset, repeated with purpose, can shatter the walls of limitation and build a foundation of unshakable growth.

Leadership is not about perfection—it is about the courage to improve, even by 5%, every single day.

The most effective leaders recognize that growth and adaptability are essential to their success, and they actively pursue opportunities for development, innovation, and transformation.

Often, what separates successful leaders from those who stagnate is not just their skill set or knowledge, but their mindset.

The **5% Rule** emphasizes small, intentional shifts in thinking that compound over time to break limiting beliefs and mental barriers.

- **Understanding the 5% Rule**

The 5% Rule is rooted in the idea that transformational change doesn't require monumental leaps overnight.

Instead, it suggests focusing on incremental improvements—small yet deliberate steps in mindset and behavior that yield substantial results over time.

Leaders who adopt this principle shift their focus from perfection to progress, allowing for sustainable growth without the overwhelm of immediate, drastic changes.

This rule challenges the "all or nothing" mentality that often paralyzes individuals.

By committing to a consistent 5% improvement in thinking or performance, leaders can unlock their potential, reframe challenges, and build resilience against mental barriers.

- **Overcoming Limiting Beliefs**

Limiting beliefs are internal narratives that confine a leader's ability to think expansively.

Common beliefs like "I'm not good enough," "I lack the resources," or "It's too late for me to change" create invisible walls that inhibit progress.

The 5% Rule tackles these beliefs by encouraging leaders to take actionable steps toward disproving them.

For instance:
- If you believe you lack the expertise to lead a team effectively, the 5% Rule suggests dedicating time daily to enhance your

knowledge or skill—whether through reading, seeking mentorship, or practicing leadership strategies.

- If fear of failure holds you back, focus on small, controlled risks that help build confidence and redefine your relationship with failure as a learning opportunity.

Every small action taken challenges the validity of limiting beliefs, gradually eroding their power over time.

- **Breaking Mental Barriers**

Mental barriers are often rooted in fear, doubt, or negative past experiences. These barriers block leaders from exploring new opportunities or implementing bold strategies.

The 5% Rule provides a framework for addressing these barriers by encouraging leaders to:

1. Acknowledge the barrier: Self-awareness is the first step to dismantling mental blocks.

2. Set small, achievable goals: Break larger objectives into 5% increments, focusing on what can be done today.

3. Celebrate progress: Each small win reinforces positive momentum and builds confidence.

For example, a leader struggling with imposter syndrome might start by acknowledging their past achievements and spending five minutes daily journaling about their strengths.

This consistent action chips away at the mental barrier, fostering a healthier self-perception.

- **Shifting Leadership Mindset**

Adopting the 5% Rule requires a commitment to three key mindset shifts:

1. From Fixed to Growth-Oriented: Leaders must embrace the belief that improvement is always possible, no matter how small the steps.

2. From Perfectionism to Iteration: Leaders should prioritize progress over perfection, understanding that mistakes are part of the growth process.

3. From Self-Limitation to Self-Discovery: Leaders who view challenges as opportunities for learning and self-improvement can better navigate obstacles.

- **Practical Applications for Leaders**

To implement the 5% Rule in your leadership journey:

1. Define your 5% improvement areas: Identify specific aspects of your mindset or performance where incremental growth is needed.

2. Create a system of accountability: Use tools like journaling, progress trackers, or accountability partners to stay consistent.

3. Seek feedback: Regular input from peers, mentors, or teams can help identify blind spots and measure progress.

4. Celebrate milestones: Acknowledging even small successes motivates continued effort.

For example, if public speaking is a challenge, focus on a 5% improvement in delivery during every presentation—whether by refining one slide, improving eye contact, or practicing for an additional five minutes.

- **The Long-Term Impact**

The 5% Rule fosters a culture of continuous improvement and resilience, essential qualities for effective leaders.

Over time, the compounding effect of small mindset shifts leads to transformational growth, enabling leaders to break free from self-imposed limitations and inspire their teams to do the same.

CHAPTER

3

LEADING FROM THE HEART AND HEAD

Imagine you are the captain of a grand sailing ship navigating uncharted waters. The **heart** is the wind in your sails, fueling your journey with energy and passion, while the **head** is the compass and map, ensuring you stay on course and avoid hidden dangers.

Now picture this: a captain who relies solely on the wind. They may start with exhilarating speed, their sails full and proud, but without a compass, they risk running aground or drifting aimlessly.

On the other hand, a captain who stares only at the compass and map, neglecting the sails, might spend hours calculating the perfect route—only to find their ship stuck in place without the energy to move forward.

To be a truly effective captain, you need both. You must feel the rhythm of the wind (heart) and harness it with intention, using the tools of navigation (head) to chart a path to your destination.

Along the way, you adjust for storms and shifting currents, combining intuition with strategy to guide your crew safely.

Your crew—your team—thrives under this balanced leadership. They see your passion and care in how you speak to them and motivate them (heart), but they also trust your clarity of direction and your ability to make sound decisions (head).

Together, you not only reach your goals but do so in a way that makes the journey itself fulfilling and meaningful.

Leadership is a complex interplay between logic and emotion. To drive meaningful change, leaders must balance decisions made with the mind—grounded in data, analysis, and strategy—with those made from the heart, which reflect empathy, values, and human connection.

This dual approach fosters trust, inspires teams, and creates a foundation for sustainable growth. Let's explore how this balanced leadership mindset enables leaders to create lasting impact.

- **The Importance of Leading from the Heart**

Leading from the heart involves showing genuine care and understanding for your team.

It is about building relationships, inspiring trust, and recognizing that every individual brings unique strengths to the table.

Leaders who engage their emotional intelligence understand how to foster an inclusive culture where people feel valued.

The connection creates a positive feedback loop, amplifying loyalty, creativity, and productivity, and driving sustainable growth and success. Key aspects of leading from the heart include:

1. Empathy in Action: Actively listening to team members, acknowledging their challenges, and offering meaningful support.

2. Purpose-Driven Leadership: Aligning decisions with core values and shared goals, making the work more fulfilling for everyone involved.

3. Emotional Awareness: Recognizing your own emotional triggers and responding thoughtfully rather than reacting impulsively.

- **The Role of the Head in Leadership**

While leading from the heart focuses on connection, leading from the head is about strategy, planning, and execution.

It necessitates a thoughtful and nuanced approach, combining critical thinking, emotional intelligence, and a deep understanding of the complex relationships at play.

Leaders must adopt a strategic mindset, assessing potential risks, allocating resources efficiently, and setting tangible, achievable goals that propel the organization forward.

This intellectual discipline ensures that passion and empathy do not overshadow practical realities.

Key aspects of leading from the head include:

1. Strategic Vision: Identifying long-term goals and outlining a roadmap to achieve them.

2. Data-Driven Decisions: Analyzing metrics and trends to inform actions and measure progress.

3. Adaptability: Staying flexible in response to challenges, pivoting strategies when necessary.

- **Finding the Balance**

Effective leadership requires a dynamic interplay between the heart and head. When decisions are made solely from the head, leaders risk appearing cold or detached.

Conversely, relying only on the heart can lead to poor planning or an inability to make tough decisions. The key lies in integrating both approaches.

Consider these strategies for achieving balance:

1. Communicate Transparently: Combine honest emotional expression with clarity about goals and expectations.

2. Practice Reflective Decision-Making: Before making decisions, evaluate both the emotional and logical implications of your choices.

3. Seek Diverse Perspectives: Encourage input from others to ensure decisions are well-rounded and consider multiple viewpoints.

- **The Impact of Balanced Leadership**

Leaders who lead with both heart and head are better equipped to foster resilience and adaptability within their teams.

They inspire confidence, not just by having a clear plan but by showing they genuinely care about the people executing it.

This balance also cultivates a culture of accountability, where team members feel empowered to take ownership of their roles.

Effective mindset change for leaders begins with self-awareness. By continuously developing emotional intelligence and sharpening analytical skills, leaders can create a harmonious blend of compassion and logic, driving positive change in their organizations and beyond.

THE EMOTIONAL QUOTIENT OF LEADERSHIP: UNLOCKING YOUR COMPETITIVE EDGE

Leadership in today's world extends beyond managing tasks and directing teams. At its core, effective leadership hinges on a leader's ability to adapt and grow—qualities that stem from a transformative shift in mindset.

The concept of emotional intelligence, or emotional quotient (EQ), has emerged as a cornerstone for fostering such a mindset.

By understanding and applying EQ principles, leaders can not only navigate complex challenges but also inspire their teams to excel.

- **The Role of Emotional Intelligence in Leadership**

Emotional intelligence is the capacity to recognize, understand, and manage emotions—both your own and those of others.

For leaders, high EQ means cultivating self-awareness, empathy, and interpersonal skills, which are essential for creating a harmonious and motivated workplace.

This methodology fundamentally changes the leadership paradigm, moving away from hierarchical command and control toward a shared, inclusive, and empowering model.

For example, consider a leader managing a team during a high-stress project. Without EQ, they may react to pressure by micromanaging or displaying frustration.

A leader with strong EQ, however, would recognize their stress signals, regulate their emotions, and communicate with clarity and empathy.

This creates a calm and focused environment, enabling the team to perform at their best.

- **Key Steps for Mindset Change in Leadership**

1. Cultivate Self-Awareness

Self-awareness serves as the cornerstone of emotional intelligence, enabling individuals to recognize and understand their emotions and behaviors.

Leaders must regularly evaluate their strengths, weaknesses, and emotional triggers.

Journaling or soliciting feedback from trusted peers can provide insights into patterns of behavior that may be holding them back.

For instance, a leader prone to interrupting others during discussions might work on active listening to foster better communication and trust.

2. Embrace Empathy

Empathy allows leaders to understand and address the perspectives and emotions of their team members.

By listening attentively and acknowledging others' emotions, leaders can create a safe, supportive environment that encourages open communication, collaboration, and conflict resolution.

For example, during a performance review, instead of focusing solely on metrics, a leader might explore the challenges an employee faced and collaboratively develop solutions.

3. Adaptability and Open-Mindedness

Mindset evolution requires a dual process of unlearning outdated patterns and acquiring new, more effective approaches to achieve personal and professional growth. Leaders should stay open to feedback, even when it challenges their views.

An adaptable mindset allows them to pivot strategies and make decisions that reflect the needs of a changing environment.

For instance, during a shift to remote work, an adaptable leader would explore innovative ways to maintain team cohesion, such as virtual brainstorming sessions or informal check-ins.

4. Focus on Relationship Building

The cornerstone of strong relationships is a harmonious blend of trust, respect, and mutual comprehension, enabling individuals to navigate life's challenges together with confidence and empathy.

Leaders should prioritize fostering genuine connections with their teams, moving beyond transactional interactions.

A leader who takes the time to celebrate small wins or remember personal milestones demonstrates care, boosting morale and loyalty.

5. Develop Emotional Regulation

Effective leaders are characterized by their ability to remain calm, composed, and focused under pressure, fostering a culture of stability and confidence within their organizations.

Emotional regulation involves pausing before reacting, reframing negative thoughts, and seeking constructive solutions.

For instance, when confronted with a missed deadline, a leader with strong emotional regulation would focus on addressing the issue collaboratively rather than assigning blame.

- **The Ripple Effect of Mindset Change**

When leaders embrace mindset change through EQ, the benefits extend beyond their immediate team.

Organizations with EQ-driven leadership often experience improved collaboration, innovation, and resilience.

When employees feel seen, heard, and valued, they become more engaged, motivated, and committed to delivering exceptional results, ultimately driving a culture of trust and high achievement.

Effective mindset change requires commitment, introspection, and consistent practice. However, the rewards—both personal and organizational—are unparalleled.

Leaders who harness EQ to navigate challenges and inspire growth set themselves apart in an increasingly competitive landscape.

By unlocking the emotional quotient of leadership, they create a lasting legacy of positive impact.

LEADING WITH EMPATHY: BUILDING MEANINGFUL CONNECTIONS

Empathy is at the heart of exceptional leadership. It bridges the gap between leaders and their teams, fostering trust, collaboration, and a shared vision.

Effective leaders understand that leadership is not merely about delegating tasks but about genuinely connecting with others to inspire and motivate.

Here, we explore how adopting empathy as a core leadership trait can drive meaningful change and create impactful relationships.

- **Understanding Empathy in Leadership**

At its core, empathy is about being present with others, actively listening to their concerns, and acknowledging their emotions with kindness and compassion.

In leadership, it means listening to your team, recognizing their challenges, and responding with care and consideration.

When leaders prioritize empathy, they build a foundation of respect and trust, enabling open communication and stronger connections.

- **Key Aspects of Empathy in Leadership:**

1. Active Listening: Empathetic leaders truly listen, without interrupting or pre-judging. They engage with their teams, seeking to understand not only what is being said but also the emotions behind the words.

2. Perspective-Taking: Empathy involves stepping into someone else's shoes to view situations from their standpoint.

Leaders who practice this gain deeper insights into their team's concerns and motivations.

3. Compassionate Action: Empathy goes beyond understanding—it's about taking action to support and uplift others.

Whether it's providing resources, adjusting workloads, or offering encouragement, empathetic leaders actively address the needs of their team.

- **The Role of Mindset Change in Leading with Empathy**

Shifting to an empathetic leadership approach requires a change in mindset. Many leaders may operate with a task-oriented focus, prioritizing results over relationships.

To lead effectively with empathy, leaders must embrace a people-first mentality.

Steps to Develop an Empathetic Mindset:

1. Cultivate Self-Awareness: Leaders must first understand their own emotions, biases, and communication styles.

By developing self-awareness, leaders acquire a deeper understanding of their own strengths, weaknesses, and emotional triggers, ultimately becoming more thoughtful, empathetic, and effective in their interactions with others.

2. Embrace Vulnerability: Empathy requires leaders to be authentic and vulnerable. Sharing personal challenges and showing genuine concern for others creates an environment of mutual respect.

3. Practice Mindfulness: Being present in the moment helps leaders to connect with their teams on a deeper level.

Mindfulness enhances emotional intelligence, making it easier to recognize and respond to others' needs.

4. Commit to Continuous Learning: Empathy is not innate; it can be developed through training, reflection, and practice.

Proactive leaders recognize the importance of feedback, using it as a catalyst for growth, innovation, and refinement of their leadership strategies to better serve their teams.

- **Building Meaningful Connections Through Empathy**

When leaders lead with empathy, they foster a culture of collaboration and trust.

Authentic connections are cultivated through mutual respect, open communication, and a shared sense of purpose, giving rise to more harmonious, productive, and fulfilling relationships.

- **Benefits of Empathetic Leadership:**

1. **Improved Team Morale:** Teams led by empathetic leaders are more engaged, motivated, and satisfied in their roles. They feel valued and supported, which boosts morale and productivity.

2. **Enhanced Communication:** Empathy promotes open and honest communication. Team members are more likely to share ideas, concerns, and feedback, creating a more dynamic and innovative environment.

3. **Stronger Team Cohesion:** Empathetic leaders nurture relationships within the team, breaking down silos and fostering a sense of unity and belonging.

4. Better Decision-Making: By considering diverse perspectives and understanding the needs of others, empathetic leaders make more informed and balanced decisions.

5. Resilient Organizational Culture: Empathy strengthens organizational culture, making it more resilient to challenges and adaptable to change.

- **Leading by Example**

Empathy is contagious. When leaders lead with empathy, they empower their teams to do the same, creating a contagious culture of compassion, kindness, and understanding that benefits the entire organization.

This positive culture reinforces a cycle of trust, respect, and collaboration that benefits everyone involved.

- **Practical Tips for Leaders:**

- **Show Genuine Interest:** Take time to learn about your team members' interests, goals, and challenges.

- **Offer Constructive Feedback:** Frame feedback in a way that encourages growth while showing understanding and support.

- **Recognize Achievements:** Celebrate successes, big or small, to show appreciation for your team's efforts.

- **Be Approachable:** Develop a team culture that emphasizes empathy, understanding, and open communication, allowing team members to share their concerns and feedback without fear of judgment or negative consequences.

- **Transforming Leadership with Empathy**

In a rapidly changing world, empathy is no longer a soft skill—it's a critical leadership trait.

By adopting an empathetic approach, leaders can drive transformation, foster meaningful connections, and create a positive and productive work environment.

Effective mindset change begins with the recognition that leadership is about people, not just performance.

By leading with empathy, leaders can unlock their team's full potential and achieve extraordinary results.

EFFECTIVE COMMUNICATION: SPEAKING WITH CLARITY AND COMPASSION

Effective communication is a cornerstone of successful leadership, especially when aiming to inspire mindset changes within a team or organization.

Leaders who master the art of speaking with clarity and compassion not only convey their messages effectively but also foster trust, understanding, and motivation among their followers.

- **Clarity: The Power of Precision**

Clarity in communication is essential for eliminating ambiguity and ensuring that your message resonates as intended. When speaking to influence mindsets, clarity involves:

1. Defining Your Purpose

Understand why you are communicating. Whether addressing a challenge, presenting a new vision, or guiding your team through change, be clear about your goals before you speak.

2. Using Simple Language

Avoid jargon or overly complex terms that may confuse your audience. Opt for straightforward, relatable language that everyone can grasp easily. This ensures that your message is accessible to all.

3. Structuring Your Message

A well-organized message is easier to follow and more impactful. Use a logical flow, starting with a strong opening that grabs attention, followed by your key points, and concluding with a clear call to action.

4. Active Listening

Effective communication is not just about conveying your thoughts and ideas; it's also about listening attentively to others, asking thoughtful questions, and seeking to understand their perspectives.

Pay attention to questions and concerns, and adjust your message to address them directly.

- **Compassion: The Heart of Connection**

Speaking with compassion requires empathy and an understanding of your audience's perspective.

This approach helps create a sense of connection, making it easier for others to embrace the changes you advocate. Compassionate communication involves:

1. Understanding Emotions

Recognize that change can evoke fear, uncertainty, or resistance. Show empathy by acknowledging these emotions and providing reassurance.

For instance, instead of dismissing concerns, validate them and explain how the change will address their needs.

2. Building Trust

Trust is foundational to mindset change. Foster open and honest communication by being your authentic self, sharing information freely, and being receptive to feedback and questions.

Share your reasons for the proposed changes and demonstrate how they align with the team's or organization's values.

3. Adopting an Inclusive Tone

Inclusive language has the power to create a sense of belonging; use it intentionally to foster a culture of respect, empathy, and connection among all individuals.

Words like "we" and "us" foster unity, while avoiding overly authoritative language encourages collaboration.

4. Showing Appreciation

Acknowledge the contributions of your team and express gratitude for their willingness to adapt. Positive reinforcement can make people feel valued and more open to change.

- **Balancing Clarity and Compassion**

To drive mindset changes effectively, leaders must balance clarity with compassion.

For example, when introducing a new initiative, clearly outline its objectives and implementation plan while empathizing with the potential challenges your team may face.

Combining these elements ensures your message is both impactful and well-received.

- **Practical Strategies for Leaders**

1. Tailor Your Approach

Different teams and individuals may require varied communication styles. Adapt your tone, language, and method of delivery to suit your audience.

2. Encourage Feedback

Cultivate an atmosphere of trust, empathy, and open communication, where team members feel comfortable sharing their thoughts, concerns, and ideas, and are encouraged to do so. This not only enriches your perspective but also builds mutual respect.

3. Practice Nonverbal Communication

Your body language, facial expressions, and tone of voice significantly influence how your message is perceived.

Create a positive and supportive interaction by using open body language, direct eye contact, and a tone that balances confidence with compassion and understanding.

4. Commit to Continuous Improvement

Continuously evaluate and refine your communication approach through self-reflection, feedback from others, and a commitment to ongoing growth and improvement.

Leadership requires ongoing growth, and becoming a better communicator is a lifelong process.

Speaking with clarity and compassion is more than just a skill; it's a leadership philosophy.

It empowers leaders to connect with their teams on a deeper level, inspire positive changes, and foster a culture of trust and collaboration.

By mastering this approach, you can guide your team through transformative mindset shifts and pave the way for lasting success.

RESOLVING CONFLICT WITH PURPOSE: TURNING TENSION INTO TEAMWORK

Imagine a team as a band of musicians tuning their instruments before a performance. Each instrument produces its unique sound—some bold like the trumpet, others soft like the flute.

But when one player's note clashes with another, tension erupts. The room fills with a chaotic cacophony, and frustration grows.

Enter the leader, the conductor. Instead of shushing the discord or forcing everyone to play the same note, the conductor listens intently to the sounds, identifying the dissonance.

They don't dismiss the trumpet's boldness or the flute's gentleness—instead, they find a way to weave the differences into harmony.

The conductor pauses, raises their baton, and speaks to the team: "What if we focused on the melody we're all here to create?"

The musicians exchange glances, realizing their shared goal isn't to outshine each other but to captivate their audience. Each begins adjusting their notes, listening to their peers, and experimenting with new rhythms.

The result? A symphony. What once sounded like tension now reverberates as teamwork.

The clashing notes become layers of harmony, each player owning their role yet contributing to something bigger. The team, once fractured, now plays as one.

This illustration mirrors how leaders can transform conflict. Like a conductor, a leader doesn't silence differences—they orchestrate them into a masterpiece, proving that with purpose, tension can fuel teamwork.

Conflict is inevitable in any team setting. Differences in perspectives, values, and approaches often create tension.

However, effective leaders understand that conflict, when approached with purpose, can lead to growth, innovation, and stronger relationships.

Resolving conflict is not about eliminating disagreements but transforming them into opportunities for teamwork and collaboration.

- **The Leader's Role in Mindset Change**

Conflict resolution begins with mindset. Leaders must shift from viewing conflict as a threat to seeing it as a chance for connection and understanding.

This requires cultivating an effective mindset that prioritizes active listening, empathy, and solution-oriented thinking.

1. Acknowledge and Validate Emotions

Tension often arises when team members feel unheard or dismissed.

Leaders who acknowledge emotions without judgment create a safe space for open dialogue.

This validation doesn't mean agreeing with all points but showing respect for differing viewpoints.

2. Seek Understanding Before Solutions

Miscommunication is a common root of conflict. Leaders should ask clarifying questions and actively listen to uncover the core issues.

This fosters mutual understanding and ensures solutions address the actual problem rather than symptoms.

3. Model Emotional Resilience

Emotions can escalate quickly in tense situations. Leaders who demonstrate calmness and self-control set the tone for others to follow.

By managing their emotions, leaders can guide the team toward productive discussions instead of heated arguments.

- **Turning Tension into Teamwork**

To effectively turn conflict into collaboration, leaders should implement strategies that encourage teamwork and mutual respect.

1. Encourage Inclusive Dialogue

Create an environment where all voices are heard. Facilitate conversations where everyone has a chance to contribute, ensuring quieter team members feel empowered to share their thoughts.

Inclusive dialogue often leads to creative solutions that may not emerge from a singular perspective.

2. Focus on Shared Goals

Highlighting shared objectives helps redirect energy from personal disputes to collective success.

When team members see how their individual roles contribute to a larger purpose, they are more likely to work together.

3. Foster Accountability and Ownership

Encourage team members to take responsibility for their actions and contributions to the conflict.

This accountability shifts the focus from blame to resolution, fostering a culture of mutual respect and personal growth.

4. Celebrate Resolutions as Wins

Recognize and celebrate moments when conflict is resolved constructively.

This reinforces the value of teamwork and motivates the team to approach future tensions with the same mindset.

- **Developing an Effective Mindset for Leaders**

Leaders must continuously develop their mindset to handle conflict effectively. Some actionable steps include:

- Practicing Self-Awareness

Reflect on your responses to conflict and identify areas for improvement. Self-awareness helps leaders recognize biases and emotional triggers that may influence their approach.

- Investing in Communication Skills

Strong communication is at the heart of conflict resolution.

Leaders should work on clarity, tone, and non-verbal cues to ensure messages are received as intended.

- Building Emotional Intelligence

Emotional intelligence (EI) is a vital trait for leaders. By understanding and managing emotions—both their own and others'—leaders can navigate conflict with confidence and compassion.

- Encouraging Continuous Feedback

Create a feedback loop within the team. When team members feel comfortable providing constructive feedback, conflicts are often addressed early, preventing escalation.

Conflict is not a barrier to success but a pathway to deeper understanding and teamwork.

Leaders who embrace conflict with a purposeful mindset can transform tension into growth opportunities.

CHAPTER

4

NAVIGATING COMPLEXITY AND CHANGE

How can leaders confidently navigate the chaos of complexity and change without losing focus or direction?

By transforming their mindset to embrace ambiguity, practice adaptive leadership, and empower their teams with a vision-driven approach.

Successful leaders see complexity not as a barrier but as an opportunity to innovate, reflect, and grow, enabling them to turn uncertainty into a strategic advantage.

The key lies in fostering resilience, emotional agility, and collective intelligence to thrive in an ever-changing world.

In today's fast-evolving world, leaders face the dual challenge of managing complexity and driving meaningful change.

Both require a mindset that not only adapts to uncertainty but thrives within it.

A leader's ability to reframe their perspective, embrace agility, and foster resilience among their teams is central to navigating these challenges successfully.

- **Recognizing Complexity**

Complexity arises when situations involve interdependent variables, where decisions are not linear and outcomes are unpredictable. Leaders must learn to:

- **Accept Ambiguity:** Instead of seeking black-and-white answers, embrace the gray areas and learn from them.

- **Break Down Systems:** Deconstruct problems into manageable components without losing sight of the bigger picture.

- **Foster Collective Intelligence:** Leverage the diverse strengths of your team to uncover innovative solutions.

- **Embracing Change**

Change is no longer occasional; it is constant. Leaders who effectively adapt their mindset to embrace transformation can turn challenges into opportunities. This involves:

- **Practicing Self-Reflection:** Recognize internal biases and assumptions that hinder growth.

- **Building Emotional Agility:** Stay flexible in your responses to challenges without being swayed by transient emotions.

- **Empowering Others:** Encourage teams to own their roles in the change process, fostering collaboration and trust.

- **Developing an Effective Mindset**

A leader's mindset is the foundation for addressing complexity and change. Transforming this mindset involves adopting strategies such as:

- **Shift from Fixed to Growth Thinking:** View failures as stepping stones to improvement rather than setbacks.

- **Cultivate Systems Thinking:** Understand how individual actions impact the broader organization and environment.

- **Adopt Adaptive Leadership:** Be willing to pivot strategies and approaches as conditions evolve.

- **Key Skills for Leaders in Transition**

1. **Resilience:** Develop mental toughness to bounce back from setbacks.

2. Empathy: Understand the perspectives of others to guide teams effectively.

3. Communication: Clearly articulate visions and expectations to inspire and align efforts.

4. Vision-Driven Action: Anchor decisions with a clear purpose to maintain focus amidst uncertainty.

Leading in the face of complexity and change requires a dynamic, adaptable mindset.

By embracing uncertainty, cultivating growth-oriented thinking, and empowering others, leaders can create a resilient organization capable of thriving in any environment.

Effective mindset change isn't a one-time event; it's a continual process of learning, unlearning, and evolving to meet the challenges of the future.

RESILIENCE AND AGILITY: LEADING IN UNCERTAIN TIMES

In times of uncertainty, leaders must develop not only resilience but also agility to navigate challenges effectively.

A leader's mindset can significantly influence how they perceive and respond to crises, shifting from survival mode to one of opportunity and growth.

This section explores how leaders can cultivate a mindset that fosters resilience and agility, empowering them to adapt and thrive in unpredictable environments.

- **Embracing a Growth-Oriented Perspective**

A growth-oriented mindset is crucial for leaders facing uncertainty. This involves viewing challenges as opportunities to learn rather than threats to stability.

Leaders who adopt this perspective focus on solutions, leverage their team's strengths, and encourage innovation.

By fostering a culture of learning, leaders can turn setbacks into stepping stones for progress.

- **The Power of Emotional Resilience**

Resilience is more than enduring tough times—it's about bouncing back stronger.

Leaders must prioritize emotional resilience by acknowledging stress and addressing it constructively.

Practices like mindfulness, reflective journaling, and focusing on controllable factors can enhance emotional stability.

When leaders demonstrate resilience, they set an example for their teams, fostering a collective ability to face challenges head-on.

- **Agile Thinking for Rapid Adaptation**

Agility requires leaders to think on their feet and adapt strategies as circumstances evolve.

This involves staying informed, remaining open to diverse perspectives, and making decisions with clarity, even when faced with ambiguity.

Agile leaders are not afraid to pivot when necessary, understanding that flexibility often leads to the best outcomes.

- **Communicating with Clarity and Empathy**

Uncertainty often breeds confusion and fear within teams. Leaders must communicate transparently, ensuring their messages are clear and empathetic.

By acknowledging challenges while focusing on actionable steps, leaders can inspire trust and motivate their teams to stay aligned with shared goals.

If you're seeking additional tools to strengthen your leadership mindset, my book **Succeeding in Hard Times** provides practical insights into overcoming adversity and emerging stronger.

It offers strategies for navigating tough situations, building resilience, and fostering the mental agility needed to lead effectively in unpredictable circumstances.

Leadership in uncertain times demands more than technical expertise—it requires a transformative mindset.

By embracing growth, cultivating resilience, staying agile, and communicating effectively, you can lead with confidence and clarity.

For deeper insights, grab a copy of **Succeeding in Hard Times** to equip yourself with actionable strategies that complement the principles outlined here.

Together, these resources will help you lead with strength and purpose, regardless of the challenges ahead.

THE POWER OF PAUSE: MINDFUL DECISION-MAKING UNDER PRESSURE

True leadership is not measured by how quickly decisions are made under pressure, but by the wisdom to pause, reflect, and act with clarity.

In the stillness of the pause lies the power to transform chaos into opportunity, reaction into strategy, and uncertainty into confident direction.

Leadership often demands quick thinking, decisive action, and the ability to navigate complex challenges.

Yet, under pressure, even the most experienced leaders can fall into reactive decision-making, which may lead to unintended consequences.

This is where the power of pause becomes a transformative tool for leaders aiming to make mindful and effective decisions.

- **The Importance of Pausing in Leadership**

The concept of pausing doesn't mean procrastinating or delaying decisions unnecessarily. Instead, it involves taking a moment to assess the situation, process information, and gain clarity before acting.

In high-pressure environments, this intentional pause can help leaders step back from emotional triggers, reduce stress, and approach problems with a balanced mindset.

Mindful leaders who practice the art of pause demonstrate greater emotional intelligence, as they are less likely to let stress dictate their decisions.

They foster better communication, build trust within their teams, and inspire confidence by showing they can handle challenges with composure.

- **How Pausing Enhances Decision-Making**

1. Clarity of Thought

Pausing allows leaders to sift through the noise and focus on what truly matters.

Instead of being overwhelmed by competing priorities, leaders can identify the core issue and ensure their decisions align with long-term goals.

2. Emotional Regulation

High-stakes situations often trigger emotional responses such as frustration, fear, or anger.

Taking a pause helps leaders manage these emotions, preventing rash decisions that could negatively impact their teams or organizations.

3. Perspective and Creativity

A moment of pause provides the opportunity to view problems from different angles.

This expanded perspective often leads to creative solutions that wouldn't emerge under a rushed mindset.

4. Strengthened Relationships

By pausing to listen actively and consider others' viewpoints, leaders show empathy and respect.

This mindful approach strengthens relationships and encourages collaboration.

- **Practical Strategies to Incorporate Pausing**

- **Breathing Techniques:** In moments of tension, deep breathing can help reset the mind and lower stress levels.

A simple practice like inhaling for four counts, holding for four, and exhaling for four can create a sense of calm.

- **Reflective Questions:** Ask yourself key questions during the pause: "What's the ultimate goal? What's the worst-case scenario? What options are available?" This helps to ground your decision-making process.

- **Step Away Briefly:** Physically removing yourself from the situation, even for a few minutes, can provide much-needed mental space to think clearly.

- **Create a Culture of Mindfulness:** Encourage your team to adopt similar practices, fostering a collective environment where thoughtful decision-making becomes the norm.

- **The Impact on Leadership Effectiveness**

Leaders who embrace the power of pause often experience profound mindset changes. They become more resilient, adaptable, and capable of navigating uncertainty.

Moreover, their teams benefit from a role model who exemplifies calm under pressure, empowering others to handle challenges with poise.

In today's fast-paced world, where instant decisions are often expected, the power of pause is a radical yet necessary practice.

INNOVATION AND RISK-TAKING: CREATING A CULTURE OF EXPERIMENTATION

True leadership is the courage to embrace uncertainty, the humility to learn from failure, and the wisdom to foster a culture where creativity thrives and risk becomes a stepping stone to progress.

It is not the absence of fear but the relentless pursuit of growth that transforms leaders into innovators and teams into visionaries.

Effective leadership requires fostering an environment where innovation and calculated risk-taking thrive.

Leaders who embrace a mindset of experimentation drive progress and empower their teams to break through traditional barriers.

Shifting your mindset to embrace these qualities involves key principles that reshape your leadership style and organizational culture.

1. Promote Psychological Safety

To encourage experimentation, leaders must create an atmosphere of psychological safety.

This means team members feel comfortable sharing ideas, even if they seem unconventional.

Establishing open channels for dialogue and eliminating fear of failure cultivates trust.

When people feel safe, they are more likely to suggest innovative solutions and take risks without hesitation.

2. Shift Focus from Perfection to Progress

Traditional leadership often emphasizes flawless execution. However, innovation thrives on the willingness to test ideas and learn from missteps.

Leaders should champion the concept of "progress over perfection," highlighting iterative development and the value of learning through action.

This shift encourages teams to focus on moving forward, even if the path includes setbacks.

3. Embrace Data-Driven Decision Making

Risk-taking does not mean acting on intuition alone. Effective leaders use data to inform their decisions while leaving room for creativity.

By analyzing trends, testing hypotheses, and evaluating outcomes, leaders can take calculated risks that are grounded in evidence.

Encourage your team to approach challenges with both curiosity and analytical thinking.

4. Lead by Example

Leadership by example is critical when fostering a culture of experimentation. When leaders demonstrate a willingness to test new ideas, admit mistakes, and pivot when necessary, it sets a powerful precedent.

By modeling an innovative mindset, leaders inspire their teams to adopt the same approach.

5. Reward Creativity and Initiative

Innovation often stems from individuals who take initiative. Recognize and reward team members who propose and implement new ideas, regardless of the outcomes.

By celebrating effort and ingenuity, leaders signal that experimentation is valued, further motivating the team to contribute their best thinking.

6. Balance Risk with Strategic Thinking

Effective leaders understand the fine line between reckless risks and strategic experimentation.

By assessing potential rewards, identifying challenges, and preparing for contingencies, leaders can take bold steps without jeopardizing their organization's stability.

Encourage teams to explore possibilities while maintaining a clear understanding of broader goals.

7. Build Resilience Through Learning

Failures are an inevitable part of innovation. Leaders must shift the narrative around failure to emphasize its role as a learning opportunity.

Conduct debriefs to analyze what worked, what didn't, and how future efforts can be improved.

Building resilience ensures the team remains motivated and forward-thinking.

8. Empower Teams with Resources

Experimentation requires time, tools, and support. Leaders should allocate resources to allow teams to explore ideas and develop prototypes.

Providing autonomy and the right infrastructure enables creativity to flourish and demonstrates a commitment to fostering innovation.

Creating a culture of experimentation is essential for leaders aiming to inspire innovation and drive transformative results.

SUSTAINABLE LEADERSHIP: CREATING A POSITIVE HERITAGE

A true leader does not chase fleeting triumphs but builds a foundation where purpose and integrity become the pillars of progress.

Sustainable leadership is not measured by the accolades of today but by the positive heritage left for tomorrow—a legacy of wisdom, resilience, and unwavering commitment to the greater good.

Sustainable leadership goes beyond achieving immediate goals—it's about fostering a legacy that benefits people, organizations, and the environment.

At its core, sustainable leadership requires a transformative mindset, one that aligns long-term vision with meaningful impact.

For leaders, achieving this involves not only cultivating their own mindset but also inspiring others to think and act differently.

- **Understanding the Mindset Shift**

Traditional leadership often focuses on short-term results, efficiency, and performance metrics.

While these are important, sustainable leadership requires a broader perspective that emphasizes adaptability, resilience, and ethical decision-making. To create this shift, leaders must move from:

1. Self-Centered Thinking to Collective Focus

Leaders need to prioritize team growth, societal impact, and shared value over individual accolades.

This requires a deeper understanding of how actions influence people and systems beyond immediate surroundings.

2. Fixed Goals to Fluid Strategies

A sustainable leader recognizes that circumstances and challenges evolve. Flexibility in approach ensures that objectives remain relevant and achievable, fostering innovation while staying grounded in core values.

3. Transactional Leadership to Transformational Engagement

Sustainable leaders focus on inspiring, mentoring, and empowering others. This shift from directing tasks to fostering creativity builds trust and commitment within teams.

- **Steps to Achieve a Mindset Change**

1. Adopt a Growth Mindset

Leaders who believe in continuous learning and improvement are better equipped to adapt to change and encourage the same in others.

Developing curiosity and openness to feedback creates a culture of learning that strengthens resilience and innovation.

2. Practice Self-Awareness and Emotional Intelligence

Sustainable leadership begins with self-awareness. Leaders must reflect on their values, biases, and motivations.

Emotional intelligence—understanding and managing one's emotions and empathizing with others—enhances interpersonal connections and decision-making.

3. Prioritize Purpose and Long-Term Vision

Leaders must clarify their personal and organizational purpose. This clarity helps align daily actions with long-term goals, ensuring decisions are sustainable and impactful.

4. Foster Inclusion and Collaboration

Sustainable leaders encourage diverse perspectives and build inclusive environments where everyone feels valued. This not only strengthens teams but also leads to more innovative solutions.

5. Commit to Ethical Practices

A sustainable mindset emphasizes transparency, accountability, and integrity.

Leaders who model these principles inspire trust and set a strong foundation for ethical behavior across their organizations.

- **Practical Tools for Mindset Change**

- **Reflection and Journaling:** Regular reflection on leadership decisions helps leaders assess their alignment with sustainability principles.

- **Coaching and Mentorship:** Engaging with mentors or leadership coaches provides valuable perspectives and guidance.

- **Team Workshops:** Facilitating open dialogues with teams fosters shared understanding and collaborative goal-setting.

- **Personal Development:** Reading, attending seminars, or joining peer networks focused on sustainable leadership can spark growth and motivation.

- **Creating a Positive Heritage**

Sustainable leaders aim to leave a legacy that inspires and empowers future generations. This means fostering a culture that values ethical growth, innovation, and resilience.

By shifting their mindset and modeling sustainable practices, leaders can create ripples of positive change that extend far beyond their tenure.

Effective mindset change for leaders isn't a one-time event—it's a journey of intentional growth.

CHAPTER 5

SUSTAINING GROWTH AND MOMENTUM

Imagine a leader as the captain of a ship embarking on a grand voyage across uncharted seas.

At the start of the journey, the waters are calm, the destination clear, and the crew full of energy.

The leader has the compass in hand—a vision that points the way. But as the voyage continues, storms roll in, the wind shifts, and the ship faces turbulent waves.

Sustaining growth and momentum on this journey requires more than just a good map; it demands an agile mindset, resilient leadership, and a crew united in purpose.

Picture this: during a fierce storm, the captain notices the sails are torn, and the compass needle seems to wobble.

Instead of panicking or blaming the crew, the captain takes a deep breath and rallies everyone.

"We may have lost the wind in our sails," the captain says, "but we have the skills and grit to steer this ship forward!"

The team improvises—patching the sails, adjusting the rigging, and even rowing when the wind dies down.

They learn to read the stars, navigate by instinct, and adapt their course to match the conditions.

The captain's mindset inspires them, transforming what could have been defeated into a new adventure of resourcefulness.

In calmer waters, the captain doesn't let complacency seep in. They encourage the crew to sharpen their skills—some learn to fish for provisions, others to repair parts of the ship.

When the crew faces a stubborn sea monster of self-doubt, the captain reminds them of their past victories, saying, "Remember the storm we conquered? If we do that, we can face anything!"

The illustration lies in this dynamic: the ship symbolizes the leader's organization, the crew represents their team, and the stormy seas embody the challenges of growth and change.

The captain's compass—their mindset—is the unshakable tool that keeps the journey alive.

Every wave, every gust of wind, and every unforeseen obstacle isn't just an enemy; it's an opportunity to navigate smarter, bond stronger, and uncover new horizons.

Just as the captain teaches the crew to trust their skills, effective leaders guide their teams to embrace challenges with enthusiasm.

They turn mistakes into maps, setbacks into stepping stones, and ordinary sailors into explorers of possibility.

By the time the ship docks at its destination, it's no longer just a vessel that completed a voyage; it's a symbol of growth, unity, and unrelenting momentum—a testament to the power of an effective mindset.

Sustaining growth and momentum in leadership requires more than just achieving milestones; it demands a continuous commitment to evolving an effective mindset.

Leaders who embrace mindset change understand that success is not a destination but a dynamic process of improvement and adaptation.

Developing this mindset involves fostering self-awareness, resilience, and the capacity to influence others positively.

To sustain growth, leaders must first shift their perspective from fixed to adaptable. An adaptable mindset allows leaders to view challenges as opportunities to learn rather than obstacles.

For instance, when a project faces delays, an adaptable leader focuses on analyzing the root cause, fostering team collaboration to find solutions, and celebrating the lessons learned rather than dwelling on setbacks.

This approach keeps momentum alive, as it builds confidence and motivates the team to continue striving for excellence.

Consistency in habits and values is another cornerstone of maintaining momentum.

Leaders must cultivate discipline in their routines and decision-making processes.

For example, regularly engaging in reflection—such as journaling or conducting debriefs after major projects—helps leaders track progress and identify areas for growth.

This habit ensures that they remain aligned with long-term goals while also staying flexible enough to adapt to new challenges or opportunities.

Resilience plays a crucial role in sustaining growth, especially in the face of adversity. Leaders with a growth-oriented mindset view failures not as endpoints but as stepping stones.

Consider a startup founder whose initial product launch underperformed due to market misalignment.

Instead of abandoning their vision, they analyze consumer feedback, refine the product, and reintroduce it with greater clarity and purpose.

Such resilience not only builds momentum but also inspires confidence in the leader's team and stakeholders.

Effective leaders also focus on empowering their teams to sustain momentum. Leadership is not a solo endeavor but a collective effort.

A leader with the right mindset understands the importance of fostering a culture of trust and collaboration.

For instance, a manager who consistently acknowledges team contributions and encourages innovation creates an environment where employees feel valued and motivated to excel.

This shared drive ensures sustained progress, as team members align their efforts with organizational goals.

Vision is another essential element in maintaining growth. Leaders who communicate a clear and compelling vision can rally their teams even in challenging times.

However, vision alone is not enough; leaders must actively connect their day-to-day actions with this larger purpose.

For example, during periods of economic uncertainty, a CEO who consistently reiterates how short-term sacrifices contribute to long-term stability helps maintain focus and morale across the organization.

Personal growth and development also underpin a leader's ability to sustain momentum. Leaders must prioritize continuous learning to remain effective in their roles.

Attending seminars, reading widely, or engaging in mentorship not only equips leaders with new skills but also sets an example for their teams.

A leader who openly embraces learning demonstrates that growth is an ongoing process, reinforcing the importance of adaptability within the organization.

Sustaining growth and momentum through effective mindset change requires a delicate balance of self-awareness, adaptability, and a commitment to collective progress.

Leaders who embrace these principles not only drive their organizations forward but also create lasting legacies of resilience and innovation.

MINDSET MAINTENANCE: BUILDING HABITS FOR LIFELONG GROWTH

How can leaders break free from limiting beliefs and foster a mindset that inspires growth and resilience?

Leaders can break free from limiting beliefs by embracing self-awareness and consistently challenging the inner narratives that hold them back.

The journey begins with identifying fixed mindsets—those that see abilities as static—and replacing them with growth-oriented perspectives, where challenges are viewed as opportunities to learn.

Through daily habits like mindfulness, journaling, and intentional goal-setting, leaders can build the mental resilience needed to navigate setbacks with confidence.

Surrounding themselves with supportive, growth-focused individuals further strengthens this mindset, while a proactive and adaptable approach ensures they thrive in an ever-evolving leadership landscape.

A leader's mindset is the foundation of their success, and maintaining it with care unlocks their full potential and inspires others to do the same.

Leadership is as much about managing one's inner world as it is about guiding others.

Effective leaders understand that their mindset—how they think, perceive, and approach challenges—shapes their success and the well-being of those they influence.

Cultivating and maintaining a growth-oriented mindset is essential for navigating the complexities of leadership.

The first step in mindset maintenance is self-awareness. Leaders need to reflect on their beliefs and assumptions to identify patterns that hinder growth.

For example, a fixed mindset—where one believes abilities and intelligence are static—can limit creativity and adaptability.

Embracing a perspective where learning and improvement are seen as lifelong pursuits fosters resilience and innovation.

This shift begins with a commitment to introspection and a willingness to challenge one's inner narratives.

Consistency is key in building habits that reinforce a positive mindset. Daily practices such as journaling, mindfulness, or setting intentional goals can help leaders stay aligned with their values and aspirations.

Journaling offers a space to process thoughts and emotions, transforming vague worries into actionable insights.

Mindfulness practices, such as deep breathing or meditation, ground leaders in the present moment, allowing them to approach challenges with clarity and calm.

Setting goals provides a clear direction, ensuring that every action is purposeful and contributes to long-term growth.

Surrounding oneself with supportive and growth-oriented individuals also plays a pivotal role in effective mindset change.

Leaders thrive in environments where feedback is constructive, collaboration is encouraged, and learning is celebrated.

By fostering relationships with mentors, peers, and even team members who embody these qualities, leaders create a network that reinforces positive habits and perspectives.

Adopting a proactive approach to setbacks is another cornerstone of mindset maintenance. Challenges and failures are inevitable, but how a leader responds to them determines their trajectory.

Viewing setbacks as opportunities to learn rather than as insurmountable barriers encourages perseverance and creative problem-solving.

This requires reframing failure as a natural and valuable part of the growth process, a mindset that inspires confidence and determination both within the leader and among their team.

Leaders must remain adaptable. The landscape of leadership is constantly evolving, requiring leaders to embrace change rather than resist it.

Flexibility, coupled with a commitment to continuous learning, ensures that leaders can pivot effectively when faced with new circumstances or unexpected challenges.

Whether through reading, attending workshops, or seeking diverse perspectives, ongoing education keeps leaders prepared and open to transformation.

THE ROLE OF A SUPPORT NETWORK: SURROUNDING YOURSELF WITH POSITIVE INFLUENCERS

A leader's true transformation begins not in isolation, but in the company of those who inspire, challenge, and uplift.

Surround yourself with individuals who reflect your potential, ignite your purpose, and hold you accountable to the greatness you aspire to become—for it is through the strength of a support network that your mindset evolves, your vision expands, and your impact deepens.

The journey of effective mindset change for leaders requires more than personal determination and self-reflection—it thrives on the power of a strong support network.

Surrounding yourself with positive influencers can transform your leadership growth into a collaborative effort, amplifying your ability to adopt new perspectives, refine decision-making skills, and maintain long-term motivation.

A support network serves as a mirror to your strengths and weaknesses, offering insights that are often difficult to recognize alone.

These influencers, whether they are colleagues, mentors, friends, or team members, provide constructive feedback that helps identify areas for growth.

By fostering relationships with those who challenge your thinking and encourage innovative approaches, you position yourself to develop a more adaptive and forward-thinking mindset.

Positive influencers do more than critique—they model behaviors that inspire change.

Observing their ability to remain resilient under pressure, communicate with clarity, or navigate challenges with creativity can ignite a desire to emulate these qualities.

Leaders can adopt new habits, attitudes, and strategies by learning from the lived experiences of others, making mindset change more actionable and attainable.

Additionally, a supportive network offers a sanctuary for encouragement and accountability. The process of changing one's mindset is rarely linear; setbacks and self-doubt are inevitable.

Positive influencers provide reassurance during these moments, reinforcing your progress and reminding you of the bigger picture.

Their belief in your potential can sustain your momentum, especially when internal motivation wanes.

The diversity of perspectives within a support network is equally crucial. Surrounding yourself with people from varied backgrounds and industries broadens your understanding of different problem-solving approaches and leadership styles.

This exposure fosters openness, a critical aspect of mindset change, and helps leaders think beyond conventional boundaries.

To cultivate an effective support network, be intentional about the relationships you nurture.

Seek individuals who align with your values, share your vision for growth, and possess qualities you aspire to develop.

Building these connections requires time and effort, but the rewards—enhanced self-awareness, expanded perspectives, and sustained personal development—are invaluable.

Surrounding yourself with positive influencers creates an environment where effective mindset change becomes not only possible but also sustainable.

As a leader, the strength of your network can shape the trajectory of your growth, helping you transform challenges into opportunities and lead with greater impact.

OVERCOMING SELF-DOUBT: STRENGTHENING YOUR LEADERSHIP CONFIDENCE

True leadership is not the absence of self-doubt but the mastery of it—transforming fear into fuel, vulnerability into strength, and uncertainty into unshakable confidence.

It is in daring to trust your own voice and stepping forward despite hesitation that you inspire others to rise, lead, and believe in the power of resilience.

Overcoming self-doubt is a pivotal step for leaders striving to strengthen their confidence and achieve transformative growth.

Leadership is not just about making decisions or driving results; it is deeply rooted in the mindset you bring to every challenge and opportunity.

The ability to trust your instincts, leverage your strengths, and remain resilient in the face of uncertainty is what separates effective leaders from those who struggle to inspire and lead with conviction.

Self-doubt often stems from internalized fears—fear of failure, fear of judgment, or even fear of success.

These thoughts can create a cycle of hesitation and second-guessing that undermines your effectiveness as a leader.

To break free, it's essential to reframe these doubts as opportunities for growth. Instead of viewing challenges as potential pitfalls, recognize them as platforms to showcase adaptability, courage, and determination.

Strengthening leadership confidence requires a deliberate shift in how you perceive your abilities.

Start by acknowledging your accomplishments and reflecting on the value you bring to your role.

Leadership confidence isn't about arrogance; it's about believing in your capacity to make a positive impact.

Practice self-affirmation by reminding yourself of past successes and the skills you employed to achieve them. This will help anchor your mindset in a foundation of competence and possibility.

Another crucial aspect of overcoming self-doubt is embracing vulnerability as a strength.

Admitting when you don't have all the answers or seeking input from others doesn't diminish your leadership; it enhances it.

This approach fosters trust and collaboration while demonstrating that confidence and humility can coexist.

By leaning into your humanity, you create an environment where others feel empowered to share ideas and support collective goals.

Effective mindset change for leaders also involves the intentional cultivation of resilience.

Setbacks and criticism are inevitable, but they don't define your worth or potential. View feedback as a tool for improvement rather than a personal attack.

Develop a habit of self-compassion, recognizing that growth comes through effort and perseverance, not perfection.

Surrounding yourself with supportive and inspiring individuals can also bolster your leadership confidence.

Engaging with mentors, peers, or a like-minded community can provide valuable perspectives and encouragement.

Their insights can help you see beyond your doubts and remind you of the broader vision you are working toward.

Overcoming self-doubt is not about eradicating all uncertainty—it's about learning to act despite it.

Leadership confidence grows when you consistently take courageous steps, however small, toward your goals.

Each step reinforces your belief in your abilities and strengthens your mindset for future challenges.

CELEBRATING SUCCESS: REINFORCING POSITIVE CHANGES

True leadership transforms not through authority, but through the celebration of progress—each acknowledgment of success becomes a spark that ignites confidence, reinforces positive change, and inspires an enduring culture of growth.

Leadership is as much about guiding others as it is about cultivating an adaptable and resilient mindset. One key aspect of effective mindset change for leaders is recognizing and celebrating success.

This act is more than just a moment of acknowledgment; it serves as a cornerstone for reinforcing positive behaviors and ensuring sustainable transformation.

Celebrating success creates an emotional connection between actions and outcomes. When leaders take the time to appreciate accomplishments, whether small or monumental, they establish a culture that values progress.

This reinforces the belief that effort and innovation lead to meaningful results, encouraging team members to adopt a similar mindset.

By doing so, leaders not only highlight achievements but also foster a growth-oriented environment.

The way success is celebrated also matters. It doesn't have to be elaborate; sometimes a genuine expression of gratitude or a thoughtfully written note can leave a lasting impact.

Tailoring celebrations to reflect the values and preferences of the team ensures authenticity, making the recognition more meaningful.

Public acknowledgment during meetings, personalized gestures, or even symbolic rewards can amplify the impact of positive reinforcement.

Leaders who celebrate success demonstrate an appreciation for both individual and collective contributions.

This act builds trust and loyalty, as people feel their efforts are noticed and valued. It also encourages others to strive for similar achievements, creating a ripple effect of positivity within the organization.

Moreover, celebrating success offers leaders a unique opportunity to anchor mindset changes.

Each celebration can be tied back to the behaviors or decisions that led to the achievement, reinforcing the new habits leaders aim to instill.

For example, if a team succeeds by embracing collaboration, highlighting this during the celebration reinforces the importance of teamwork as a critical value.

Celebrations also contribute to a leader's personal transformation. When leaders make recognition an integral part of their approach, it fosters humility and mindfulness.

They become more attuned to the strengths and efforts of others, cultivating a mindset rooted in appreciation rather than solely results-driven metrics.

In the pursuit of effective mindset change, celebrating success is a powerful tool. It turns victories into learning opportunities, reinforces desired behaviors, and strengthens the bond between leaders and their teams.

CHAPTER 6

THE FUTURE OF LEADERSHIP

Leadership is no longer just about authority and decision-making power; it's about adaptability, vision, and, most importantly, mindset.

The future of leadership demands a shift from the traditional, hierarchical models to one that nurtures innovation, empathy, and emotional intelligence.

As we look ahead, leaders will need to embrace change not just in systems or structures, but within themselves.

This requires a complete transformation in the way leaders think, act, and interact with their teams and the world.

Leaders must cultivate a mindset that not only adapts to change but also thrives in uncertainty.

In a world increasingly driven by technological advancements, globalization, and shifting societal values, the future of leadership hinges on the ability to lead with resilience, agility, and an open mind.

The key to this transformation lies in an effective mindset change—a recalibration of how leaders perceive challenges, setbacks, and growth opportunities.

Throughout history, we've seen leaders emerge who defied traditional leadership paradigms. One such figure is Mahatma Gandhi, who transformed the world not with force but with a mindset of nonviolence, self-discipline, and empathy.

His leadership was rooted not in controlling people but in inspiring them to change themselves.

Gandhi's success lay in his belief that to lead others, you must first transform your own mindset to reflect the values and vision you wish to instill in others.

In the 20th century, business leaders like Steve Jobs and Elon Musk reshaped industries by daring to think differently.

These visionaries embodied what it meant to lead with a transformative mindset.

Jobs challenged conventional wisdom by focusing on the design and user experience rather than simply the product's technical specifications.

Musk revolutionized space exploration and electric cars, not by relying on outdated leadership models but by adopting a forward-thinking mindset that embraced risk, creativity, and a relentless pursuit of the future.

These historical examples underscore a critical lesson: true leadership is not about simply holding power or maintaining the status quo. It is about the ability to adapt, innovate, and evolve.

The future of leadership is intrinsically tied to this mindset shift, one that views challenges as opportunities and believes in leading by example.

As we step into the future, the traditional mindset of leadership—focused on authority, control, and top-down decision-making—will continue to lose relevance.

In its place, a new era of leadership will emerge, defined by flexibility, continuous learning, and shared responsibility.

Leaders will be expected to foster environments where innovation flourishes, diversity is celebrated, and every team member feels empowered to contribute their ideas.

To achieve this, leaders must undergo a profound transformation in how they view their roles.

Effective mindset change involves moving away from the belief that leadership is about having all the answers, and instead recognizing that it is about fostering collaboration, encouraging creativity, and supporting personal growth.

Leaders of the future will focus on servant leadership, where they prioritize the needs of their team and work toward helping individuals develop their own leadership potential.

This shift requires a deep understanding of emotional intelligence—empathy, self-awareness, and the ability to manage relationships.

Leaders will need to be both compassionate and strategic, able to balance the needs of their people with the demands of their organizations.

This type of leadership involves active listening, the willingness to learn from others, and a readiness to adapt to new information and perspectives.

Moreover, as the pace of change accelerates, resilience will become a cornerstone of effective leadership.

Leaders who embrace a growth mindset—believing that challenges are opportunities for learning and development—will be best equipped to navigate uncertainty.

They will lead not from a place of fear or control but with the confidence that comes from their ability to adapt and pivot when needed.

The future leader will be one who inspires trust by being authentic, transparent, and open to feedback.

They will create a culture where failure is not feared but seen as an essential part of the learning process.

In doing so, they will inspire their teams to take calculated risks, embrace innovation, and pursue excellence with a sense of shared purpose.

The future of leadership is not about clinging to outdated models or rigid structures.

It is about embracing the power of mindset transformation—shifting from a focus on authority and control to one of collaboration, resilience, and empathy.

Leaders who can make this change will not only lead their organizations to success but will also shape a future where leadership is defined by its ability to inspire, innovate, and create lasting positive change.

As we continue to face unprecedented challenges and opportunities, those who cultivate an effective mindset change will stand out as the leaders who will lead us into the future.

THE EVOLVING LEADER: STAYING RELEVANT IN A RAPIDLY CHANGING WORLD

In a world where the only constant is change, leaders must evolve or risk becoming obsolete. Staying relevant isn't about merely adapting to trends—it's about embracing a transformative mindset that propels individuals and organizations forward.

Leadership is no longer confined to authority or expertise; it's about resilience, adaptability, and a forward-thinking approach.

As a leader, your mindset isn't just your internal compass—it's the framework through which you navigate challenges, inspire your team, and create meaningful impact.

But how can leaders foster this transformative mindset? How can they cultivate habits and perspectives that drive innovation and sustainable growth in a rapidly shifting environment?

Here are key strategies to build an effective mindset for leaders in the modern age:

1. Adopt a Growth-Oriented Perspective

Effective leaders prioritize learning over perfection. They understand that mistakes are not failures but opportunities to grow.

A growth-oriented perspective encourages curiosity, fosters creativity, and eliminates fear of failure. Instead of asking, "Why did this happen to me?" ask, "What can I learn from this?"

Practical Tip: Dedicate time weekly to learn something new—be it a skill, a concept, or an industry update.

Engage in active reflection on your progress to ensure continuous improvement.

2. Focus on Emotional Agility

Leadership today requires not just intellectual capability but emotional intelligence.

Emotional agility enables leaders to manage their feelings effectively, remain calm in crisis, and build stronger connections with their teams.

Practical Tip: Practice mindfulness to increase self-awareness and manage stress.

Develop active listening skills to understand the emotions and concerns of others, making your leadership empathetic and impactful.

3. Challenge Fixed Assumptions

Leaders who cling to old paradigms often find themselves outpaced by competitors who think differently.

A critical part of mindset evolution is challenging fixed assumptions and seeking fresh perspectives.

Practical Tip: Regularly engage with individuals from diverse backgrounds and fields. Their viewpoints may challenge your own and spark innovation.

4. Embrace Uncertainty as Opportunity

In volatile times, fear of uncertainty can paralyze leaders. Effective leaders flip the narrative, viewing uncertainty as fertile ground for new possibilities. This mindset empowers them to navigate ambiguity with confidence.

Practical Tip: Use scenario planning to envision different outcomes and prepare strategies for each, building confidence in your ability to face the unknown.

5. Commit to Servant Leadership

An evolving leader prioritizes the needs of their team and organization above their own.

By focusing on serving others, leaders can inspire trust, loyalty, and collaboration, which are essential for navigating change.

Practical Tip: Actively seek feedback from your team and implement changes that align with their needs. This demonstrates a commitment to collective growth.

6. Develop Resilience Through Adaptability

Resilience doesn't mean resisting change—it means adapting to it. Leaders with adaptable mindsets recover quickly from setbacks, pivot when necessary, and maintain focus on long-term goals.

Practical Tip: Break complex challenges into smaller, manageable tasks. This approach helps you maintain momentum and avoid burnout during tough times.

7. Cultivate a Visionary Mindset

Visionary leaders don't just react to change—they anticipate it.

They think strategically about the future, recognizing trends and opportunities before they become apparent to others.

Practical Tip: Dedicate time to forward-thinking activities, such as trend analysis or brainstorming sessions, to keep your vision sharp and relevant.

Mindset change isn't a one-time event; it's an ongoing journey. Leaders who commit to growth, adaptability, and emotional intelligence will not only stay relevant but thrive in the face of disruption.

As the world continues to evolve, the question isn't whether change will happen—it's whether you're ready to lead through it.

Now is the time to rethink your approach, challenge your perspectives, and embrace the future with confidence.

The leaders who succeed aren't those who resist change, but those who harness its power to create a legacy of innovation and impact.

LEADING WITH PURPOSE: ALIGNING MINDSET WITH CORE VALUES

Leadership is more than a position—it's a responsibility to inspire, influence, and guide others toward a shared vision.

At its core, effective leadership begins with the right mindset, one that is purpose-driven and anchored in unwavering core values.

But how do leaders transform their mindset to lead with clarity, authenticity, and impact?

- **The Power of a Purpose-Driven Mindset**

Imagine leading a team through uncertainty, where every decision you make has the potential to inspire confidence or sow doubt.

Leaders who thrive in these moments are not just skilled strategists; they are guided by a strong sense of purpose.

Purpose gives leadership depth—it turns actions into meaningful contributions and motivates teams to rally behind a cause greater than themselves.

- **Aligning Mindset with Core Values**

To lead effectively, your mindset must align with your core values. Core values act as a compass, guiding decisions and interactions.

Without this alignment, leaders risk appearing inconsistent or insincere, eroding trust with their teams.

When mindset and values are in harmony, leaders project authenticity, fostering loyalty and respect.

- **Clarity in Decision-Making:** Leaders with purpose are decisive because they know their values.

This clarity reduces hesitation and ensures every decision aligns with long-term objectives.

- **Building Trust Through Authenticity:** Teams follow leaders who are genuine. Aligning your mindset with your values demonstrates integrity, making you a leader people can rely on.

- **Resilience in the Face of Challenges:** Core values are an anchor in turbulent times. They provide the strength to navigate setbacks without compromising principles.

- **Practical Steps for Mindset Change**

1. **Identify Your Core Values:** Start by reflecting on what truly matters to you. Values like integrity, innovation, or empathy are the foundation of your leadership.

2. Evaluate Your Current Mindset: Are your daily actions aligned with these values? Assess areas where your mindset may need adjustment to better reflect your principles.

3. Adopt Purposeful Practices: Cultivate habits that reinforce your values. For instance, if empathy is a core value, schedule time to genuinely listen to your team.

4. Seek Feedback: Ask trusted peers or team members to provide insights on how your leadership aligns with your stated values. Their perspective can be invaluable for growth.

5. Lead by Example: Consistently demonstrate your commitment to your values in both words and actions. Leadership is not about perfection but about striving to live your principles every day.

- **Transforming Leadership Through Mindset**

Changing your mindset is not a one-time event; it is an ongoing process of growth and self-awareness.

Purpose-driven leaders continuously evaluate and refine their approach, ensuring their leadership remains relevant and impactful.

CREATING A MINDFUL LEADERSHIP CULTURE: INSPIRING POSITIVE CHANGE

In a world where leadership defines the trajectory of teams and organizations, the most transformative leaders are those who embrace change—not just in strategy but within themselves.

Leadership isn't about holding a title; it's about nurturing a mindset that empowers others, inspires action, and adapts to challenges with clarity and purpose.

To cultivate a culture of mindful leadership, it begins with a fundamental shift: changing how leaders think, respond, and lead.

- **Why Mindset Matters in Leadership**

Your mindset shapes your actions, and your actions shape the culture around you. Leaders with a growth mindset—those who believe that abilities and talents can develop through dedication and hard work—create environments where innovation thrives, resilience grows, and people feel valued.

In contrast, a fixed mindset fosters rigidity, fear of failure, and a lack of creative exploration.

Leadership success today demands a mindful approach, where self-awareness, emotional intelligence, and intentional decision-making are at the forefront.

When leaders embrace this perspective, they don't just lead—they inspire transformation.

- **Steps to an Effective Mindset Change**

1. Cultivate Self-Awareness

The journey begins with looking inward. Leaders need to identify their own biases, assumptions, and thought patterns that might limit their growth or negatively influence their teams.

Self-awareness enables leaders to understand their impact and make intentional choices aligned with their values.

Action Step: Dedicate time daily to reflection, journaling, or mindfulness practices to deepen your understanding of your strengths and growth areas.

2. Adopt a Learning-Oriented Mindset

Leaders who embrace a mindset of continuous learning are better equipped to adapt to changing circumstances.

This means staying curious, being open to feedback, and viewing challenges as opportunities rather than obstacles.

Action Step: Seek out perspectives different from your own—whether through books, discussions, or professional development programs.

3. Master Emotional Intelligence

Mindful leadership is rooted in the ability to understand and manage emotions—both your own and those of others.

Emotional intelligence builds stronger relationships, fosters trust, and ensures calm, measured responses during crises.

Action Step: Practice active listening and empathy. Make it a priority to understand the emotions behind your team's words and actions.

4. Foster Resilience

Mindset change isn't a one-time event—it's a process that requires resilience.

Resilient leaders view setbacks as learning moments and bounce back with renewed determination.

They model perseverance, showing their teams how to navigate uncertainty with strength and grace.

Action Step: Develop habits that promote resilience, such as setting boundaries, maintaining a balanced perspective, and celebrating small victories.

5. Prioritize Vision and Purpose

Effective leaders align their mindset with a clear sense of purpose. When leaders are purpose-driven, their actions become intentional, their teams feel inspired, and their culture evolves into one of collective growth.

Action Step: Regularly revisit and refine your vision. Ensure it reflects your core values and communicates a clear, inspiring path forward.

- **Inspiring Positive Change in Others**

Leaders who undergo mindset transformation set the tone for their teams. They become role models for adaptability, accountability, and continuous improvement.

When leaders prioritize their mindset, they unlock the potential to create a ripple effect—one where positive change becomes contagious.

Inspiring change in others requires trust, authenticity, and a commitment to empowering those around you.

Rather than dictating behaviors, mindful leaders ask meaningful questions, encourage collaboration, and celebrate the journey of growth.

- **Leadership as a Daily Practice**

Mindset change is not a destination; it's a daily practice. Every decision, interaction, and response offers an opportunity to lead mindfully and inspire positive change.

As a leader, your greatest legacy lies not in the achievements you secure but in the people you uplift and the culture you shape.

THE MINDSET LEGACY: SHARING YOUR WISDOM WITH FUTURE GENERATIONS

Leadership is a journey that evolves as the world changes, but at its core, it requires the ability to adapt, inspire, and leave a legacy of impact.

For leaders, mastering mindset change is not just a skill—it's a legacy that shapes future generations.

Here, we delve into actionable strategies for effective mindset transformation, enabling leaders to guide their teams with clarity, purpose, and resilience.

1. Understand the Power of Self-Awareness
Effective mindset change begins with self-awareness. Leaders must examine their own beliefs, biases, and habits.

This introspection allows them to recognize patterns that hinder growth and identify opportunities for improvement.

Self-awareness fosters humility, a crucial trait for leaders to connect with others authentically and inspire trust.

2. Embrace a Growth-Oriented Perspective

A growth-oriented perspective focuses on possibilities rather than limitations. Leaders who cultivate this mindset view challenges as opportunities for innovation.

By fostering a learning culture, they encourage their teams to embrace adaptability, resilience, and creative problem-solving.

3. Lead by Example with Emotional Intelligence

Mindset change requires emotional intelligence—the ability to understand and manage emotions effectively.

Leaders who demonstrate empathy, self-regulation, and clear communication inspire their teams to adopt these qualities.

Emotional intelligence bridges gaps, resolves conflicts, and strengthens team cohesion.

4. Practice Consistent Reflection and Adaptation

Leaders thrive by continually reflecting on their decisions and adapting their approaches.

Regular reflection helps leaders align their actions with their core values and long-term goals.

This practice ensures that their mindset remains flexible and responsive to evolving circumstances.

5. Create a Vision that Resonates

Vision is the foundation of leadership. A compelling vision inspires action and fuels mindset change.

Leaders must articulate their vision in a way that connects emotionally with their teams.

This clarity empowers individuals to see their role in achieving shared objectives, fostering alignment and purpose.

6. Foster Collaborative Growth

Leadership isn't about individual achievement; it's about empowering others.

Effective leaders invest in their teams' development, offering mentorship and opportunities for growth.

By fostering a collaborative environment, they create a ripple effect of positive mindset changes throughout their organizations.

7. Celebrate Progress, Not Perfection
Mindset transformation is an ongoing journey. Leaders who celebrate small victories reinforce positive behavior and encourage continuous improvement.

Recognizing progress over perfection reduces fear of failure, boosting confidence and motivation among team members.

8. Leave a Legacy of Empowerment
True leadership leaves a legacy. Leaders who focus on empowering others create a culture that thrives beyond their tenure.

CONCLUSION

Leadership is not merely about managing tasks or guiding teams—it is about inspiring change, both within yourself and those you lead.

The essence of effective leadership lies in the ability to shift your mindset, breaking free from limiting beliefs and embracing the endless possibilities of growth and innovation.

A transformed mindset doesn't just influence outcomes; it reshapes the culture, vision, and destiny of your team and organization.

Great leaders are those who dare to step beyond comfort zones, embracing challenges as opportunities to evolve.

They recognize that every decision, every action, and every thought has the potential to drive progress or stifle it.

By cultivating resilience, fostering empathy, and committing to continuous learning, leaders can unlock their full potential and ignite the potential in others.

As you move forward in your leadership journey, remember this: the most significant change begins within.

The mindset you adopt today will shape the legacy you leave tomorrow. Lead boldly, think expansively, and act with purpose.

In doing so, you won't just lead effectively—you will inspire transformation that lasts for generations.

The time to shift your mindset and elevate your leadership is now.

THE MINDSET REVOLUTION: TRANSFORMING LEADERS, TRANSFORMING ORGANIZATIONS

Leadership isn't just about strategies or results—it's about perspective. The most successful leaders understand that transforming their mindset is the key to unlocking greater possibilities, both for themselves and their organizations.

But how do you move from simply managing people to inspiring transformation? It begins with embracing a new way of thinking that empowers growth, resilience, and innovation.

- **The Power of Perception**

Imagine this: two leaders face the same challenge, yet one sees it as a threat, while the other views it as an opportunity for growth.

What makes the difference? Their mindset. Mindset governs how leaders approach problems, engage with teams, and adapt to change. It's the invisible force that shapes decisions and outcomes.

For leaders, shifting from a fixed mindset—where challenges are seen as insurmountable barriers—to a growth-oriented mindset is the first step toward transformational leadership.

This isn't just self-help jargon; it's a critical skill backed by decades of research.

Leaders with a growth mindset actively seek feedback, prioritize collaboration, and innovate fearlessly, creating a ripple effect throughout their organizations.

- **Strategies for Mindset Change**

1. Cultivate Self-Awareness

Effective leadership begins with knowing yourself. Leaders must be honest about their strengths, weaknesses, and mental roadblocks.

Reflection and feedback from trusted peers or team members can illuminate blind spots and open doors to personal growth.

2. Adopt a Learning-Oriented Approach

In a world of constant change, leaders who prioritize learning over perfection inspire creativity and resilience in their teams.

Whether it's learning from mistakes or staying curious about industry trends, leaders who model a commitment to growth inspire the same in others.

3. Focus on Empowerment, Not Control

Leaders often fall into the trap of micromanaging, stifling creativity and independence. A mindset shift toward empowering teams fosters trust, encourages collaboration, and ignites innovation.

When leaders see themselves as enablers of success rather than controllers of processes, teams thrive.

4. Embrace Adaptability

The ability to pivot during uncertainty is the hallmark of great leadership. Leaders who adapt their mindset to accept change as a constant can turn crisis into opportunities, positioning their organizations for long-term success.

- **Transforming Organizations Through Leadership**

Organizations mirror their leaders. When leaders transform their mindset, the cultural shift is palpable. They build workplaces where psychological safety, innovation, and accountability thrive.

Teams are more motivated when they see their leaders lead with humility, integrity, and a focus on growth.

This isn't just theory—it's actionable. Studies show that organizations led by growth-minded leaders see higher employee engagement, increased profitability, and stronger adaptability to market changes.

Leaders set the tone; their mindset becomes the foundation upon which organizational success is built.

The mindset revolution isn't a trend; it's a necessity. The future of leadership demands flexibility, empathy, and a willingness to embrace change.

As a leader, the question isn't whether you can transform your mindset—but whether you're willing to.

The transformation of organizations begins with individuals like you, ready to lead not just with authority but with vision and adaptability.

The time to change your perspective is now. Are you ready to join the revolution?

ABOUT THE AUTHOR

Scott E. Salsbury is a well-regarded author and leadership expert focused on helping people and organizations reach their highest potential.

With a Doctorate in Psychology, Scott uses his deep understanding of human behavior to create practical solutions for leadership, personal growth, business, and financial success.

Scott has worked alongside various international organizations, designing targeted training programs to strengthen leadership and promote individual growth.

His fresh, effective approach has motivated countless leaders, encouraging trust and teamwork across all levels.

In his books, Scott combines relatable stories with practical strategies that give readers the skills they need to thrive in today's demanding business world. His philosophy centers on the idea that real leadership is rooted in authenticity and the ability to inspire others.

Known as a respected voice in his field, Scott shares his insights through speaking engagements, workshops, and one-on-one coaching, building a community of empowered leaders ready to tackle tomorrow's challenges.

BOOKS OF THE AUTHOR

1. Path to purposeful leadership
2. Leading with trust and teamwork
3. Succeeding in hard times
4. Succeeding with goal challenges
5. Transforming self criticism into self compassion
6. Mindful living essential
7. The essential guide to power and influence
8. The skills that shape success
9. The path to influence and persuasion
10. Insight into the power of behavior
11. Success Habits For Aspiring Leaders
12. Skills for motivating teams effectively

www.ingramcontent.com/pod-product-compliance
Lightning Source LLC
Chambersburg PA
CBHW052149220526
45471CB00004B/1596